DASHAVATARAM

JOURNEY THROUGH THE 10 LEGENDARY INCARNATIONS OF LORD VISHNU

OSHEEN

Made with ♥ on the Notion Press Platform
www.notionpress.com

To my beloved parents,
for their endless love, guidance, and encouragement.

To all the young readers,
may these stories inspire you to believe in goodness, bravery, and the
power of faith.

And to Lord Vishnu,
whose divine avatars remind us that good always triumphs over evil.

With love,
Osheen
(Author, 10 years old)

Contents

Foreword

It is with immense pride and joy that we write the foreword for Dashavataram, the third book of our daughter, Osheen, who at just 10 years old has already shown a deep love for storytelling and a remarkable understanding of our rich cultural heritage. Osheen's journey as an author began when she was just 8, with her first book, Ramayan, and continued at age 9 with Adventure with the Sea and The Sand, a delightful tale of her own adventure. Now, with Dashavataram, she brings to life the ten incarnations of Lord Vishnu, exploring their significance with both innocence and wisdom.

What amazes us the most is not just her ability to write, but her passion for learning and sharing these timeless stories with other young readers. It is rare to see such dedication and creativity at such a young age, and We couldn't be prouder of Osheen for her accomplishments.

This book is a reflection of her growing curiosity and her connection to our spiritual and cultural roots. We hope Dashavataram will inspire all who read it, especially children, to appreciate the beauty of these ancient tales and the values they hold.

As parents, we are incredibly grateful to witness Osheen's journey, and we look forward to seeing her continue to dream, create, and share her stories with the world.

With love and pride,
Gopal Krushna Sahu/Sarmistha Pattanaik
(Father and Mother of Osheen)

Preface

I am delighted to share my book, Dashavataram, which tells the stories of the ten powerful incarnations of Lord Vishnu. These divine forms, known as avatars, appear on Earth whenever there is a need to restore balance and protect goodness. Each avatar has a unique story filled with lessons of bravery, wisdom, and compassion.

The journey of this Book started from a calendar where I found the pictures of 10 incarnations of Lord Vishnu. I am fascinated by these pictures and made a promise to draw these pictures in my drawing book. Soon I took interest in knowing the details about the 10 incarnations of Lord Vishnu.

As a young reader and writer, I found myself fascinated by these stories, not just for their adventure and excitement, but also for the deep values they teach us about life, faith, and the eternal fight between good and evil. In writing this book, I have tried to present these timeless tales in a way that is easy for other children like me to understand and enjoy.

And finally, it materialized into a Dashavataram my 3rd Book.

I hope Dashavataram inspires everyone who reads it to learn more about the great epics of our culture and discover the lessons hidden within them. It has been a joyful journey for me to explore these stories, and I look forward to sharing that joy with you.

I apologize to you for any mistakes or errors in this book. I am too young to edit myself but I promise you will try to improve when I grow up a little more.

With love and gratitude,

Osheen

(Author, 10 years old)

Acknowledgements

First and foremost, I would like to thank my parents for always supporting and encouraging me in everything I do. Their belief in me gave me the confidence to write this book.

I am also grateful to my teachers, who have inspired my love for stories and helped me learn so much about our rich cultural heritage.

A big thank you to my friends, who always cheer me on and motivate me to do my best.

Lastly, I express my deepest gratitude to Lord Vishnu, whose stories of Dashavataram have filled my heart with awe and wonder. This book is my humble effort to share these timeless tales with the world.

Lots of thanks to Notion Press Publishing Platform for making book publishing so easy that a 10-year KID like me can write and publish a Book without any fee. I am looking forward to publishing my future books in Notion Press.

With love and thanks,
Osheen

Prologue

This book is about the ten avatars of Lord Vishnu. It tells us how a tiny fish which could fit in your palm, grows bigger than the biggest ship. It tells us how a God rescues Mother Earth from a demon. This book is filled with amazing history which you might have never heard before. So, if you want to discover the past in these hidden pages of the book, this book is the best for you.

1

Matsya Avatar

1. INTRODUCTION

The rule of the Earth is quite simple. There are four Yugas- Satya Yuga, Treta Yuga, Dwapar Yuga and Kali Yuga. These four Yugas together form a Chatur Yugar and 100 Chatur Yugas form a Kalpa. After each Kalpa, Lord Vishnu takes birth on Earth and does the destruction of the whole world but saves the ones who follow the path of Dharm and righteousness. Such a Kalpa was about to end. Destruction has already started in one part of the Earth. Lord Vishnu was calmly sleeping on Sheshnaga with Goddess Lakshmi sitting beside him. Goddess Lakshmi politely tried to wake up Vishnu by saying "Lord, one Kalpa has ended. Destruction has already eaten one part of the Earth. Every creature, human, animal, and tree is perishing. You must bring your devotees and the ones who are righteous to safety. Oh Preserver, save your helpless devotees". Lord Vishnu smiled and closed his eyes.

2. THE INCARNATION OF MATSYA AVATAR

Suddenly something shone on his forehead and a fish (Matsya in Sanskrit) originated before Vishnu and Lakshmi. A radiant light shone from the eyes of Vishnu which crafted the fish and the fish turned into the colour of gold. Goddess Lakshmi bowed before the first incarnation of Lord Vishnu. During that time, the most blessed devotee of Lord Vishnu and the best man of dharma and righteousness was King Satyavrat. Lord Vishnu first thought of the idea of testing Satyavrat.

The next morning, when King Satyavrat finished his morning prayer in the sea and was just about to put the water of the sea, which was, in his cup of hands he heard a tiny voice "Please save me!". The voice was coming, from the water in King Satyavrat's cup of hands. Satyavrat was taken back by surprise. Satyavrat saw a very small fish in his hands which was actually Matsya Avatar about which King Satyavrat didn't know. The fish said, "King, I am a very small fish. There are very large waves in this sea and the big fish are a big threat to me. I have many chances of dying here. Please save me!". King Satyavrat was very kind and felt pity for the fish. Satyavrat said "Don't worry dear fish, I will take you to the palace and ensure that no harm comes to you." The fish said, "Thank You, King, Thank You!". Satyavrat put the tiny fish gently in his container of sacred water and took the fish to his palace.

King Satyavrat soon reached his palace chanting Om Vishnu, Om Narayana. He kept the container on a table and got dressed in royal garments and precious jewellery. Suddenly he heard the sound of splattering water. He saw the container shaking and he moved closer to see what was happening. He saw the fish growing into a bigger fish than the previous state. The fish cried "Save me!". King Satyavrat was shocked at this quickly growing of the fish. He rushed with the fish and put it in the aquarium. After some time a very loud clattering sound was heard and Satyavrat rushed to see what was happening. The aquarium was broken into small pieces and a big fish was struggling for breath. King Satyavrat was so surprised he nearly fell down. He exclaimed, "What! Now this fish was smaller than my palm and now it is bigger than this large aquarium".

The fish cried "Save me, Save me!". King Satyavrat picked up the fish and rushed to his royal pond. Satyavrat put the fish in the pond and was about to leave when the fish spoke "King, King, Please don't leave me! I am very scared. What if something happens to me? Kindly stay here!". Satyavrat said, "Oh don't worry, I will stay with you here. I am resting here and I will take care of you". The fish said, " That's so generous of you king, thanks". Satyavrat sat on one royal chair and closed his eyes wanting to take some rest. Just then the sound of the gurgling of water was heard which broke King Satyavrat's sleep. He looked into the pond and saw the fish growing into a very large fish and struggling for breath. It cried "Save me. This place is too small for me. Save me!". The surprised king took the fish and rushed to the giant sea and put the fish in the water.

3. VISHNU TAKES HIS REAL DIVINE FORM

The King watched with eyes wide and mouth open as the fish began to grow 50 times bigger than King Satyavrat. Satyavrat said, "Oh my God! What a sight! Humanity must never have seen such a large creature. Oh Vishnu, Oh Preserver, Oh Narayana, What maya am I seeing?". Suddenly the fish (Matsya avatar) vanished and in place of the fish stood The Preserver of the World, The one whose finger carries the Sudarshan Chakra, Lord Vishnu. King Satyavrat's eyes nearly popped out. He fell at the feet of Vishnu and said "Oh Lord, I have earned the goal and purpose of my life by meeting you". Vishnu said, "King Satyavrat, I am very pleased by your devotion and your walk towards dharma. You took my care and I am very satisfied but I want to you ask you for something". Satyavrat replied after bowing down "Lord, I will lay down my life for you. I will try my best and achieve the thing you want me to. Kindly ask".

Vishnu smiled and said "Satyavrat, if you know, one Kalpa has ended. Destruction has already started. I want you to build a large boat and put all kinds of creatures, animals, insects, herbs, trees, humans, etc. You must put all living things in the boat. Bring the saptarishis and your family and servants too. Bring my dear Vasuki with you too in the boat and don't worry I will help you". Satyavrat said, "As you wish Lord".

4. CONSTRUCTION OF THE BOAT

From the next day, the construction of the large boat started. All of the best workers and servants were summoned and put to work. Messengers were sent far and wide to gather everyone as instructed by Vishnu. Woods were being cut and poles were constructed and put in the boat. Slowly, the boat began to take shape. With each day and each night, the boat improved a little bit and more and more passengers began to come. At last, the day dawned for which everyone was waiting. Satyavrat made everyone sit in the boat including his family and servants but was the last one to enter the boat keeping the most priority about others.

When he entered the boat he said "Where did Vasuki go? Has he not come yet?". Satyavrat's servants said, "King we told him to assemble here. He is late". Satyavrat said, "Let's wait for him". His servants said together "No king, let's close the door of the boat. Otherwise the sea water will enter the boat and everyone will drown". Satyavrat said, "How can we be so heartless to Shri Vasuki. Lord Vishnu had said to bring Vasuki on the boat. I have full faith in him. He will surely come". Just then Vasuki appeared and got seated on top of the boat. The servants closed the door and the boat started sailing on the dangerous waves of the sea.

5. MATSYA LEADS THE PATH

The boat was big but however, couldn't control the waves of the giant sea. The boat kept tossing up and down, side by side and the passengers were getting very scared. King Satyavrat consoled everyone by saying "Don't worry. Have full faith in god. Lord Vishnu will surely come. He will surely save us. Just then everyone saw the Matsya by the window of the boat. Everyone bowed down and prayed. Lord Vishnu came in his actual form and said "King Satyavrat, you have done a wonderful job. Nobody shall worry. I will lead your path". The Matsya (avatar) led the path and the passengers were relieved and reassured. They now had nothing to worry about.

6. JAMBUDWEEP

The next morning when everyone looked out the window they saw large mountains covered with snow. The saptarishis said, "This mountain is Jambudweep." All the others nodded in agreement "Yes, yes!". When they reached the shore of the mountain Jambudweep, they got out of the boat and thanked Lord Vishnu for helping them. Thus, this was how Lord Vishnu took the form of Matsya and saved his devotees.

Test Your Knowledge

Q1. How many Yugas are there in the world?

a. 1
b. 5
c. 4
d. 10

Q2. A fish is called Matsya in which language?

a. Hindi
b. Sanskrit
c. Tamil
d. Telugu

Q3. How did King Satyavrat bring the small fish to his palace?

a. In his container of sacred water
b. In a bowl
c. In a plate
d. In an aquarium

Q4. What did Lord Vishnu tell King Satyavrat to make?

a. A ship
b. A house
c. A palace
d. A large boat

Q5. Which snake was seated on the top of the boat?

a. Vasuki
b. Sheshnaag
c. Anaconda
d. King Cobra

2

Kurma Avatar

1. INTRODUCTION

One pleasant morning, the holy sage Durvasa was strolling in the forest when he saw a beautiful apsara flying in the sky holding a very beautiful garland of flowers. The flowers were of different colours and their smell filled the surroundings. Durvasa addressed the apsara "Beautiful apsara, will you give me this wonderful garland of flowers?". The apsara stopped and said, "Of course, it will be my honor to give you this garland". The apsara gave the garland and flew away as Durvasa continued walking with the garland. Soon, he saw Indra with his followers, servants, and the devas (gods). Durvasa gave the wonderful garland to Indra and said "Respected Indra, I find you the one fit to be worthy of this beautiful garland of beautiful flowers". Indra took the garland but wanting to make fun of the moment, threw the garland on the head of his elephant, Airavata. Airavata on his side trampled it with his trunk then threw the garland on the ground, and stepped on it destroying the beautiful garland. Seeing this Durvasa became very angry. His eyes became large and his mouth uttered a terrible curse "Indra, today you and your Airavata dishonored me and because of this fault of yours, you as well your followers shall suffer. Your Airavata elephant will also be lost. From today, you Indra, and all devas of all elements will lose all their powers, jewellery, and shine. You all will also lose your crowns and you will suffer".

2. LORD VISHNU'S PROPOSAL

Indra and the devas roamed around and finally went to Lord Vishnu with Lord Brahma. All the devas and Indra bowed down before Vishnu and Indra said "Narayana, please save us. Sage Durvasa's curse has robbed us of our powers, crowns, jewellery, shine, glory, and wealth. How long can we remain on like this? We really want to get rid of this curse. Please save us, Lord, please save us". Vishnu smiled and replied "Devas, for this you have to take out Goddess Lakshmi from the ocean and please her and for this, you all need to do the churning of the ocean, Kheersagar". All the devas gasped and said together "What! Churning of the large ocean? Will we ever be able to do it?". Vishnu said "Of course not, there are not that many devas who will be able to do the churning. We will need the support and help of the asuras too".

Indra asked "Asuras! Will they even accept our request and by the way they can cause a lot of trouble. They will also ask us for some of the belongings that will emerge from the ocean". Vishnu said "Then you will share some with them.

Their king Bali will accept the offer and come to help and yes, Amruta will also come out". Indra said "Amruta! Amruta, the liquid that is drunk by someone makes the person immortal. But, the demons will also ask for it as of their share of the churning". Vishnu said "Eventually you should. But if the demons consume Amruta, then the world will be in great trouble. You do one thing. You all devas go to the Asuras and ask them for their help. Also, mention that Lord Vishnu has asked them to join the devas. Tell them that they will get some belongings and Amruta will also come out". Indra said "But they will drink the.......". Vishnu interrupted "I will take care of that". All the devas bowed and with Indra, they marched right to the Asuras.

3. CHURNING OF THE OCEAN

At last, the final day dawned of the churning. Nobody had ever seen such a sight before. Devas and Asuras working together. They started the churning with the Mountain Mandara as the churning pole and the serpent, Vasuki as the churning rope. The Asuras formed a straight line with their king Bali in the front. The devas did the same with Indra in the front. The asuras grabbed the head of Vasuki while the devas grabbed the tail. The two groups stood straight and were ready. Then, the asuras and devas started churning. They used all of their power and worked very hard.

However, there was a big problem. The more they churned the more the mountain Mandara went deeper into the sand. The devas lost control and fell many times in the water. Actually they all were standing in the water and doing the churning but the devas fell by losing balance and the asuras laughed merrily at them. Bali shouted, "Indra fell down. Agni fell down. Vayu fell down. Varuna fell down. Surya fell down". The demons laughed. The gods were very angry. After some time, the asuras too fell down but this time the gods did not laugh due to their good attitude. Soon, the gods and asuras fell many times. Mount Mandara went deeper and deeper into the sand and the gods as well as Asuras were losing balance. Soon, Mount Mandara went half into the sand and all the gods prayed to Lord Vishnu. The demons again laughed at their helplessness. The devas prayed and prayed.

4. KURMA HOLDS THE MOUNTAIN

At last, Vishnu accepted their prayer. A radiant light shone from Vishnu's face and formed a spark-like star. It went to the place where the churning was going on. There the light changed into a turtle (Kurma in Hindi). The devas saw Vishnu in the turtle. All the gods bowed before the second incarnation of Lord Vishnu, Kurma avatar, and sang prayer. Bali shouted, "The gods bowing down before a mere turtle". Roars of laughter came out of the asura's mouth. The devas simply ignored them. Mountain Mandara was going deeper into the sand and Indra said "Kurma avatar, save us!".

By this time, the Asuras and Bali were fed up. Bali said "I knew there was no point coming here and wasting time in here. The gods came to us and asked for our help for their own benefit. However, it was only our fault for coming here. Hey all asuras, let's go out of here. Move out!". They started walking back as the Kurma went in the water and went under the sand. It carried the mountain on its back and swam up. The asuras turned back to see what was happening hearing the sound of splashing of water. To their utter amazement, Mount Mandara was coming back to it's position as Kurma was holding it on his back. The asuras came back to their position, and the devas and the asuras together resumed churning of the ocean.

5. LORD SHIVA DRINKS THE POISON

The churning of the ocean was once again resumed and continued till another problem arose. Due to the churning of the ocean, the most destructive poison in the world Halahal came out of churning. The poison spread everywhere and the devas and the asuras coughed, and Indra shouted in panic "Halahal has risen and has started spreading. If it spreads completely it has the power of destroying the whole world. The world is in danger. We all will die". All the devas prayed to Vishnu for a solution. Vishnu materialized before them and said, "This is not in my power. For this, you have to ask Lord Shiva. Only he can get you rid of this destructing situation". All the devas and asuras together prayed to Lord Shiva. Lord Shiva stood up from his seat and raised his hand forward. Goddess Parvati rushed and came there and asked "What are you going to do Lord?". Shiva said, "I am going to drink the poison Halahal". Parvati said, "What! You are going to drink Halahal? No! I will not let you do it!".

Shiva calmly turned towards Parvati and said "Parvati, why are you stopping me?". Parvati said, "What do you mean, my Lord? You are going to drink poison and you expect me not to stop you?". Shiva held Parvati's hands and said "Parvati, I am the saver of the world. My duty is to protect the world. Don't worry about me. Nothing will happen to me". Reassured, Parvati allowed Shiva to do so. Shiva gathered his hands and all the Halahal poison came to his hands and he drank the poison. The universe resembles in Shiva, if the poison went down under Shiva's neck, the whole world would be in trouble. So the poison stayed in the neck of Lord Shiva and he soon after got another name, Neelkantha (The Blue- Throated One). The whole world was saved now and all the devas and asuras prayed to Shiva and thanked him. So, the problem of Halahal was over.

6. MATERIALS EMERGE FROM THE OCEAN

Again the churning of the ocean was resumed and continued. After churning and churning, finally, lot many materials slowly began to emerge from the ocean. First, precious gems came out which were shared by both asuras and devas. Then, Kamadhenu, the holy cow was gifted to the sages. After that, a very big precious diamond which was green in colour was obtained which was nearly an Emerald. The devas wanted to gift it to Vishnu but the asuras insisted the diamond be given to them. Bali, King of the Asuras, said "I agree with the devas. It was only because of Lord Vishnu that we are successfully doing the churning. Let's give the diamond to Lord Vishnu". So, the diamond went to Lord Vishnu and peacefully settled on his necklace.

Three beautiful apsaras came out. The asuras shouted, "We want them! We want them!". Bali said, "You foolish Asuras, our goal is Amruta, not apsaras!". So, the apsaras went to the devas (gods). Then Kalpavriksha, The Wish- Fulling Tree, was obtained which went to Indra's garden in heaven. Parijat which was a special tree for its flowers always shone, also went to Indra's garden. Afterwards, Airavata, Indra's elephant was also found which was given to Indra. Then, Varuni, a beautiful apsara came out with a pot of alcohol. The asuras shouted, "We want this!". Varuni poured the alcohol down into the mouths of the delighted asuras. Bali shouted, "Our goal is only Amruta, not anything else".

Next, Goddess Lakshmi came out. The devas prayed and Lakshmi gave them their crowns, wealth, shine, glory, and power back but the asuras said

"What a beautiful woman! We want this girl! This woman is ours!". The gods shouted, "Don't invite our wrath asuras. She is Goddess Lakshmi. Treat her with respect! Bali, control your asuras, or else, your asuras can be in danger". Bali replied, "Why? Not only the gods have a right to the belongings. The asuras also should get them. So there's no fault in my asuras to ask for". Rahu, a asura asked Lakshmi "Beautiful woman, will you marry me? If yes, I will be your slave forever!". Another asura shouted, "No, she is mine". Lakshmi said, "I do not belong to anyone. My husband is Shree Vishnu and I don't want to desire anyone else". The asuras said, "We don't care. Why desire the one who is not here? Tell us, where is Vishnu? Tell us!". Lakshmi thought 'Oh Vishnu, why are you testing me so much? You know, I am here, where are you?'.

Parvati went to Vishnu and bowed before him. Vishnu also bowed and asked the reason for the sudden visit. Parvati said, "During my wedding to Lord Shiva, you performed the rites of a brother. So, that makes you my beloved brother". Vishnu smiled mischievously "Then, that also makes you my sister!". Parvati said, "Brother! Lakshmi is waiting for you. Now will you go or.......". Vishnu said, "Okay, I am going. Actually, I was only waiting for my sister! Let's go". Vishnu and Parvati disappeared and went to Lakshmi. The asuras were continuously asking Lakshmi to marry them. Vishnu went there and married Lakshmi and took her away. Next, Uchchaishravas, a very beautiful and magnificent horse that was white in color came out. Seeing the Asuras losing patience for Amruta, Indra gifted the horse to Bali.

Then something came out that was so shiny that the devas and asuras were forced to close their eyes. When the gods and demons tried to see what was the thing, they saw the moon. The light was so shiny that the waves of the ocean began to rise. The devas and asuras prayed to Lord Shiva and Shiva appeared. He said "My greetings to you, Shree Narayana" to the Kurma avatar. The kurma changed into Vishnu and he said "My hearty greetings to you, Dev of Devas, Mahadev". Shiva smiled and the moon god, Chandrama bowed down before him. Chandrama changed into moon and he settled on Lord Shiva's matted hair. After that, the most awaited thing came out.

The god of Ayurveda, Dhanvantari came out with herbs, Vedas, and a golden vessel in which contained Amruta. Before Dhanvantari could speak something, Rahu, an asura with another asura snatched the vessel from Dhanvantari's hand and they both flew away to Patallok, the place where asuras stay. All the asuras including Bali ran after them and the devas shouted "Stop! Stop otherwise the result will be too bad for you!". But the asuras were nowhere to be seen. They had already flown away to Patallok.

7. THE MOHINI FORM

Indra said "I knew this asuras would surely snatch Amruta from us. At least, we have got our powers back from Goddess Lakshmi. Let's run after the asuras to Patallok. We won't let the asuras drink Amruta at any cost". Vayu dev said "But till we reach, they must have already consumed Amruta ". Indra said "But we can't just stand here and do nothing". Saying so, all the devas rushed to Patallok. Back there, Lakshmi said to Vishnu "Lord, it's time for your Mohini form". Vishnu smiled "As your wish!". Again, a radiant light shone from Vishnu, and a female, Mohini, stood before them.

Lakshmi joined her palms before the Mohini form of Lord Vishnu. Mohini was so beautiful that anyone could fall into her trap of beauty. Mohini flew to Patallok. All the Asuras were running after Rahu. Mohini whispered "Why are you in such a hurry Rahu ji?" in her sweet enchanting voice. Rahu stopped and the moment he looked at Mohini, he stood straight. Mohini slowly took away the vessel of Amruta from Rahu. Soon all the asuras gathered there and everyone was so enchanted by her beauty that nobody cared about the vessel of Amruta anymore. Bali asked mesmerized "Who are you, beauty?". Mohini replied, "My name is Mohini". Bali asked, "What are you doing here in Patallok?". Mohini replied, "I have come here to distribute Amruta among all of you. King Bali, you are the king of asuras, so the first right of the Amruta goes to you.

Here, I will pour Amrita into your hands. Drink it". Mohini was just about to pour Amrita into Bali's cup of hands when a loud voice was heard "Stop devi". It was Indra. All the devas rushed in. Indra said, "We can't let the Asuras drink!". Mohini asked "Why not?". She turned back and all the devas saw Lord Vishnu in her. All the gods joined their palms. Bali shouted, "Devas! Don't try to take away Mohini from us. She has come for us". Mohini turned towards Bali "Yes, King Bali. You said fully correct. I have come for you all asuras". The asuras shouted to the devas "We will drink the Amruta first!". The devas shouted back "And we will never let you do it!". Soon all the devas and asuras started arguing loudly.

Mohini said "Silence!". She turned towards the asuras and said "Have any of you ever tasted Amruta?". Nobody said yes. There was pin-drop silence. All the asuras paid full attention to Mohini. Mohini said "So, listen to me. When Amrita is being prepared, the Amrita on the above part is not the actual tasty, boiled, and yummy Amruta. The real Amruta is in the below part. So, let the gods consume the upper part of Amruta and then you will consume the real Amruta". Bali asked "But why are you helping us?". Mohini smiled "Because the devas have always done injustice to you". The asuras asked "Are you sure that there will be Amruta left for us too?". Mohini smiled "Of course!". "The asuras were truly happy. They were completely unaware about the fact that they had fallen into the trap of Lord Vishnu.

8. RAHU AND KETU

The next bright morning, the asuras and devas formed two different lines. Mohini first went to Indra and gave him a portion of Amrita. As soon as he drank it, his body shone like a jewel. Slowly, slowly Mohini served all the devas their portion of the Amruta. When Mohini poured Amruta into the hands of the last deva, Surya dev (The Sun God) and Chandrama (The moon god) shouted "He is not a deva! He is an asura!". As soon as these words were spoken, the last deva in the line changed into Rahu. Bali shouted "Rahu?". Rahu laughed out loudly "Ha! Now no one can kill me! I am immortal!". Mohini whispered, "You betrayed me?". Rahu said, "Yes! Betrayed! The day I first looked at you, I sensed something strange. I knew you would cheat us asuras".

Mohini became very angry and the Sudarshana Chakra appeared on her finger. The Chakra flew and cut Rahu's head but he was already immortal. Rahu was very angry with Surya Dev and Chandrama. He said "Surya dev and Chandrama! You are the cause of my head being cut. From today, my head will be known as Rahu and my body will be called Ketu. I will sometimes eclipse you Chandrama with my head and sometimes you too Surya dev with my body". After all that, all the Asuras were very angry about being betrayed by Mohini and the Devas. A battle followed between the asuras and the devas in which the victory went to the devas which was obvious as the devas had consumed Amruta.

Test Your Knowledge

Q1. What did Durvasa see in the sky?

a. An apsara holding a beautiful garland of flowers
b. A king riding a magical horse
c. A god flying after an asura
d. Dark clouds in the sky

Q2. Who trampled the beautiful garland of flowers?

a. Indra
b. Airavata
c. Varun Dev
d. Agni Dev

Q3. What was the name of the ocean which they churned?

a. Arctic Ocean
b. Indian Ocean
c. Kheersagar
d. Atlantic Ocean

Q4. Lord Vishnu took the form of a very beautiful woman. What was her name?

a. Lakshmi
b. Parvati
c. Durga
d. Mohini

Q5. Who snatched the vessel of Amrita from Dhanvantari?

a. Bali
b. Indra
c. Rahu
d. Ketu

3
Varaha Avatar

1. INTRODUCTION

Varaha avatar took place in Satya Yuga. It all started when the Sankadik rishis went to Vaikuntha to meet Lord Vishnu. The Sankadik rishis were the 4 sons of Lord Brahma and were great rishis. Although they were older in age, they liked to stay in the form of children's rishis all the time using their divine powers. Because of that, they were also called Baal (children) rishis. There are 7 doors before you can enter Vaikuntha and meet Lord Vishnu. The 4 rishis had crossed the 6 doors and were at the 7th door when the guards of Vaikuntha and Lord Vishnu, Jaya, and Vijaya stopped them. They said, "You can't go in!". The children rishis asked, "Why?". Jaya said, "See, you are children. You haven't even introduced yourselves. Meeting Lord Vishnu is not a simple and easy thing. You should go and play with toys".

One child Rishi said "See, I am Sanat, he is Sanatan, his name is Sanandan and he is Sanatkumar. Our four brothers are the Sankadik rishis. We mean no harm to you but just want to take the blessings from Lord Vishnu. Please let us go in". Vijaya found a nice excuse to stop them "Lord Vishnu is taking rest. We just can't let you in". The 4 children rishis said "Ok. No problem. Don't worry. We will wait for Lord Vishnu to wake up". Saying so, the Baal rishis sat down in meditation.

Many days passed. Jaya said to Vijaya "Many days have passed but these four don't even take the name of going out of here". Vijaya shouted, "Hey children, we said that go and play with toys". The four Baal rishis stood up and Sanat said "Respected Jaya and Vijaya, please let us go in. We want to meet Vishnu". Jaya got irritated "You are very stubborn and naughty children. We said you can't visit means you can't!". Sanatkumar said "Stop!". Vijaya said, "You stop talking! How many times I have told you that you all can't meet, can't meet. Just get out of here and play with toys. If you want, we can provide you with a very tasty and delicious meal".

The Sankadik rishis got very angry. Sanandan said, "Enough! You have insulted us too much! We asked you politely but you don't deserve that". The four Baal rishis took water from their holy container and Sanatan said "Today, we all curse you both that you no longer will stay as the guards of Shree Vishnu". Sanat said, "You don't deserve to stay close to Lord Vishnu. Therefore, we curse you that you both will take births as humans on Earth and go through the circle of life and death". Saying so, the four rishis threw the water on Jaya and Vijaya. Jaya and Vijaya looked at each other. They were truly scared. Suddenly, the 7th door, the universe, everything vanished.

2. 3 BIRTHS AS ENEMIES

The Sankadik rishis as well as Jaya and Vijaya found themselves standing near Lord Vishnu. Goddess Lakshmi said, "Sankadik rishis, it's a pleasure to meet you. We welcome your arrival". Sanandan said, "We are very pleased at having met you and Lord Vishnu. Now, we have your blessings forever". Vishnu smiled "I greet you Baal Rishis". Sanatkumar said "Our hearty greetings and wishes to you, Lord". Jaya and Vijaya said to Vishnu "The Baal rishis gave.......". Vishnu interrupted and turned towards the Sankadik rishis and said "I am really sorry on behalf of my guards for their extremely bad behavior towards you". Sanatan said, "Oh Lord, please don't say these things. You are making our hearts small. Jaya and Vijaya didn't do it on purpose. They did it unknowingly". Vishnu smiled and turning towards Jaya and Vijaya said "Yes, due to their curse, you have to leave Vaikuntha and go to Earth and stay as humans".

Jaya and Vijaya asked tears rolling down their eyes "But, how can we leave you for so many days Lord?". Then turning towards the Sankadik rishis, Jaya requested with folded hands "Baal rishis please take away your curse. We request you with folded hands. We really don't want to stay away from Lord Vishnu". Sanat replied thoughtfully "We are extremely sorry but we can't take away the curse as we being the Sankadik rishis once given a curse to someone can't take it back as it is not in our power". Vishnu said, "Yes, what they are saying is true". Vishnu, seeing Jaya's and Vijaya's sad faces, said "However, I can give you two options". Jaya and Vijaya looked with hope. Vishnu said, "You can take 7 births as my blessed devotees or 3 births as my enemies. After this period of births, you both will come back to Vaikuntha and reunite with me. The choice is yours". Vijaya said, "Lord, we can't stay without you for so long, for 7 births". Jaya said, "So, we have decided that we will stay 3 births on Earth even if we have to be your enemies and we have to be killed by you". Vishnu smiled "Tathastu (as your wish in Sanskrit)".

3. TROUBLE AROUND THE WORLD

Soon after that Sage Kashyap's wife, Diti, became pregnant. After a period of time, Diti gave birth to two baby sons. One was named Hiranyaksha (who was Vijaya) and the other was named Hiranyakashipu (who was Jaya). It was their first birth as enemies. Hiranyaksha was the smaller one while

Hiranyakashipu was the elder brother. When the both of them grew up, with their asura names, they also began to cause trouble around the world. Hiranyaksha being the smaller brother, killed people, animals, sages, etc mercilessly. He was always eager about war. He took his soldiers and destroyed forests, villages, palaces, and everything that came before him.

Thousands of people were killed by him. He was also very powerful. He killed his enemy's soldiers single-handedly. The world was fed up by his wrong- doings. Once, a group of sages were doing meditation and praying to Lord Vishnu around the holy fire. Hiranyaksha with his soldiers destroyed the Yagna and killed some of the sages. Those who were alive said, "Oh Vishnu, Oh Preserver, save us. Save this world from Hiranyaksha". Suddenly, Hiranyaksha thought 'Why not go to Swargloka and conquer Indra Dev? Also, I can test my power'.

4. DEFEATING INDRA

The next morning, he went to the gates of Heaven and shouted outside the door "Indra, open the door. Open!". When nobody opened the door, Hiranyaksha burst through the door with his powerful legs. Indra Dev was ready with his Vajra (Indra's weapon). Hiranyaksha fought with Indra. Indra Dev put up a good fight but Hiranyaksha defeated him (but didn't kill him) easily and went away laughingly. Having lost Swargloka, the devas did not know where to go. Then Varuna Dev (The God Of Water) took all the devas and Indra Dev to his abode, Varunalok.

Hiranyaksha was too angry on Varuna. He went to Varunalok with his weapon, two sharp swords. All the devas froze from head to toe after seeing Hiranyaksha. Varuna and Indra were the most scared. Hiranyaksha pointed at Varuna and shouted, "Varuna, how dare you give shelter to Indra after I have defeated him? You have invited me for a fight by doing this thing. Come and fight with me. Come!". Varuna walked away from the devas but closer to Hiranyaksha. Indra tried to stop him but Varuna already went near Hiranyaksha. Hiranyaksha asked, "Are you ready?". Varuna said, "Hiranyaksha, after defeating Indra Dev, you have gained control over all the devas including me. So, you have no point in fighting with me. I am no match for you".

Hiranyaksha gave up an evil smile "So, you accept defeat?". Varuna looked down "Yes". Hiranyaksha laughed out loudly "Ha! Ha! Ha! There is no one in this universe more powerful than me". Varuna said looking up confidently "There is". Hiranyaksha became angry. He kept one of his swords on Varuna's neck. Varuna felt very scared. Hiranyaksha snarled "Who is he?". Varuna smiled "Shree Hari, Shree Vishnu. The Preserver.". Hiranyaksha asked, "How does he look? Where does he live?". Varuna said, "Wait. He will come to you.

Bhoodevi is troubled by your evil doings. Shree Hari will come to save Bhoodevi from you". Hiranyaksha went away laughingly "Let him come. I will defeat him like I defeated you. Ha! Ha! Ha!". After he went away, a very evil thought came to his mind "Why not throw Earth (Bhoodevi) into the waters in which once somebody enters can't come out? If I do this, Bhoodevi will no longer be able to provide food to the devas and all the devas as well as Bhoodevi will be in extreme danger and Shree Vishnu will surely come to fight with me and save Earth (Bhoodevi)".

5. BHOODEVI PRAYS FOR HELP

Hiranyaksha flew outside the Earth. He began to increase his size. When he stopped increasing, it seemed as if a million Earths would fit inside him. Goddess Bhoodevi, dressed in white, looked fearfully at Hiranyaksha. She knew that she was in trouble. Hiranyaksha slapped Earth (Bhoodevi) so hard that Earth flew away and bounced and came back again to the hands of Hiranyaksha. Mother Earth (Bhoodevi) was very scared. She cried for help. All the devas were seeing the sight, very scared. Hiranyaksha laughed then looked here and there. He noticed the waters in which once somebody enters can't come out. He threw Bhoodevi into the water. Bhoodevi fell into the water at great speed. Mother Earth cried "Oh Vishnu, help me. Now, you are only my hope. Save me, help me". All the devas prayed to Lord Vishnu with folded palms.

6. KILLING OF HIRANYAKSHA

Goddess Lakshmi said to Lord Vishnu "Lord, Bhoodevi is in danger. Please have mercy on her and save her". Once again, a radiant light shone from Lord Vishnu's necklace and a Man- Boar who was blue in color came out. Lakshmi bowed before the 3rd incarnation of Lord Vishnu, Varaha Avatar. The Varaha had 2 long, sharp, and pointed tusks. He had a head like a boar's head and a human's body. He had a long garland on his shoulders and looked like Vishnu as he was Vishnu's avatar. He flew at great speed towards the water in which Bhoodevi had fallen. Hiranyaksha saw the creature and shouted, "Hey! Where are you going? Oh, so you are Shree Hari. Go, go inside the waters and you will never be able to come out again".

Varaha went inside the waters. He came out again with Bhoodevi on his tusks. He flew towards one direction. Hiranyaksha flew after him shouting "Hey, Hari. You creature, you will pay for this! Where are taking Earth? She is mine!". Varaha continued flying and kept Bhoodevi back in her position in the universe. Mother Earth bowed down before Varaha and Varaha smiled. Then turning towards Hiranyaksha Varaha said, "I am Shree Hari, Lord Vishnu. I have had enough of your wrongdoings. You wanted to fight with me right? Come on Hiranyaksha, fight!". All the devas bowed before Varaha. Hiranyaksha rushed towards Varaha with both of his swords. Varaha caught Hiranyaksha's hands threw his swords away and pushed him back. Hiranyaksha was very surprised and frightened at Varaha's power. But he threw a large rock towards Varaha which broke into pieces as soon as it touched Shree Varaha's body.

Hiranyaksha could not believe his eyes. He again rushed towards Varaha but as soon as he touched Varaha's body he fell down. He tried one more time with greater force. Varaha caught Hiranyaksha's shoulders. Hiranyaksha was very scared. Varaha went closer to Hiranyaksha's face and cut Hiranyaksha's head with his sharp tusks. The head flew away. The remaining body was left which Varaha let go of his hands. Then he kicked the body with all his might. All the devas and Bhoodevi bowed down before the Varaha incarnation of Lord Vishnu. When Hiranyakashipu got his younger brother's head, he became very angry. He took a vow "I will kill that creature who killed my beloved brother".

Test Your Knowledge

Q1. The Sankadhik rishis were the sons of which God?

a. Lord Shiva
b. Lord Vishnu
c. Indra Dev
d. Lord Brahma

Q2. How many doors are there before entering Vaikuntha?

a. 7
b. 5
c. 4
d. 10

Q3. What is 'as your wish' called in Sanskrit?

a. Tathastu
b. Chiranjivi Bhava
c. Viksham Dehi
d. Matsya

Q4. What is Indra Dev's weapon?

a. A sword
b. Vajra
c. Bow
d. Spear

Q5. With what did Varaha Avatar cut Hiranyaksha's head?

a. Sudarshan Chakra
b. Knife
c. His tusks
d. Sword

4
Narasimha Avatar

1. INTRODUCTION

Hiranyakashipu loved his brother, Hiranyaksha very dearly. Hiranyakashipu was so angry with Lord Vishnu for killing Hiranyaksha that his heart boiled with rage for Shree Vishnu. He was in the court of his palace. He shouted, "I will kill that Vishnu". Guru Shukracharya, Guru of the asuras said "Don't take it that easily, Hiranyakashipu. Hiranyaksha was very powerful but Lord Vishnu finished him so easily. Lord Vishnu is the Preserver Of The World. He is invincible. Killing him is not as easy as you think. Hiranyakashipu said thoughtfully "Yes, Hiranyaksha was so powerful that he conquered heaven and defeated Indra Dev but Vishnu killed him.

Tell me, Guru, what should I do?". Shukracharya said, "My advice is that you should go and meditate and please Lord Brahma. When he appears, you should ask him elixir, Amrita, the liquid of immortality". Hiranyakashipu smiled and said "Nice idea!". Hiranyakashipu went to his wife, queen Kayadhu and said "Dear, I am going deep into the forest to meditate and please Lord Brahma and ask him Amrita to fight with Vishnu". Kayadhu said sadly "Is it necessary for you to go? Please don't leave me and go away. Plus, you don't know that I am pregnant now.

I will soon be giving birth to a child". Hiranyaksahipu wiped Kayadhu's tears and said "Don't worry, Kayadhu. You are the queen. You have to keep calm. I am so happy with the good news". Kayadhu said "But don't you want to enjoy the birth time of our son in happiness in our grand palace? Please don't leave me". Hiranyakashipu said "It's very important for me to go. You stay comfortably in the palace. I will go but I will return soon". Saying so, Hiranyakashipu went to the forest to do meditation.

2. HIRANYAKASHIPU GETS A BOON

Hiranyakashipu followed very strict rules and meditated very seriously. He stood on top of a big rock and meditated on one leg and kept the other leg above the ground. He prayed and meditated for many, many days. There in heaven, Indra Dev decided to take the opportunity. He shared the evil thought with his ministers, the gods "Let's go and kidnap Kayadhu, wife of Hiranyakashipu. We should take this opportunity and be ready for action. I have heard that Hiranyakashipu has gone deep into the forest for meditation. I have also heard that Kayadhu is pregnant. After we kidnap Kayadhu, she will give birth to a child. And after that, we will immediately kill the newborn baby".

Some gods opposed the killing of an innocent, just a newborn baby but Indra insisted so the gods carried out with the idea. Indra kidnapped Kayadhu but when the Narada intervened and said that killing Hiranyakashipu's and Kayadhu's child may bring destruction to the gods, Indra was panicked. He left Kayadhu in Narada's ashram and ran for his life in heaven. Kayadhu wore the dresses of women's sages, orange color sarees. Narada told the women of the ashram to take good care of Kayadhu. Kayadhu lived happily in the ashram for many days. She listened to the music of the praises of Lord Vishnu every day. She was adjusted to that and she was happy for the pleasant life.

3. PRAHLAD IS BORN

The baby in Kayadhu's womb was also listening to the music of Lord Vishnu everyday sang by Narada and the sages and women sages in the ashram. The baby also sang in the womb. Lord Vishnu smiled. He had already chosen his devotee. There deep in the forest, Lord Brahma was pleased with Hiranyakashipu's devotion and finally appeared. Brahma said, "I am very pleased with your devotion and meditation. Ask for a boon, Hiranyakashipu". Hiranyakashipu said without a thought "Give me the elixir Lord Brahma". Brahma said calmly "Hiranyakashipu, if you know the rules of the universe. I can't give Amruta to anyone. If you wish for something else, ask for it. You can also give conditions for your death to make your death time after a very long period".

Hiranyakashipu shouted immediately "Then what is the use of praying to you for so many days if you can't give me what I wish for?". But then with an evil smile, Hiranyakashipu said "Okay, I agree. This is my wish. Listen carefully". Thunderstorms gathered and lighting struck when Hiranyakashipu said these words "Not in a day, not at night, Not inside, not outside, Not on Earth, not in the sky, Not by gods, not by animals, Not by men, not with any weapons I can be killed! This is my wish". Brahma smiled "Tathastu (as your wish in Hindi)".

Back in Narada's ashram, Kayadhu gave birth to a baby boy. He was very cute and Narada held the baby in his hands. A small wooden cradle was made for the baby decorated with flowers. The cradle was put outside the houses, on the road of the ashram, and the baby was kept in the cradle. Kayadhu was bright with happiness. She asked to Narada "Great rishi, you are one of the wisest. Can you tell the future of my dear child? Can you say what will my son become in the future?". Before Narada could reply, a loud voice was heard "He will be my heir and the future king of my kingdom".

Kayadhu, Narada, and all the sages turned back. It was Hiranyakashipu and his army Hiranyakashipu said "Kayadhu, I am back". Kayadhu ran towards Hiranyakashipu and touched her husband's feet. Hiranyakashipu said with pride "Bring my son". Kayadhu gave the newborn baby to his father. Hiranyakashipu was very happy. He caressed his son lovingly. Holding the baby, Hiranyakashipu turned towards Narada. Hiranyakashipu said, "Devarshi, I am so thankful to you for saving my wife and giving her shelter". Narada smiled "It's nothing, King. It was my duty".

Hiranyakashipu said, "Kayadhu, let's go back to our palace. Guru Shukracharya will name our child". Kayadhu said, "Husband, let Devarshi Narada give our son a name. He saved my life. Because of him, our healthy son is born". Hiranyakashipu agreed and asked "Devarshi, kindly give the most appropriate name to my beloved son". Narada said, "His name will be Prahlad and he will bring glory to the world". Hiranyakashipu said "Prahlad. What a wonderful name! This name suits my heir, my son. Saying so, Hiranyakashipu raised Prahlad and caressed him. Hiranyakashipu went back to his palace with his wife (Kayadhu) and son (Prahlad). After a few days, Hiranyakashipu went away to conquer the whole world with his large army.

4. PRAHLAD COMES BACK FROM GURUKUL

Hiranyakashipu went to Swargloka and conquered heaven. He went to create trouble around the whole world. His hatred towards Vishnu was so much that he punished everyone who was a devotee of Lord Vishnu. After chaining all the sages and people who were devotees of Lord Vishnu, he chained Indra and all the devas. Then he took them to a large place and placed his asura soldiers behind them. The asuras held a large sword. Then Hiranyakashipu went up a little stairs and everyone noticed a very large thing covered with red cloth. Hiranyakashipu took off the cloth and there stood a very large metal statue of Hiranyakashipu.

Hiranyakashipu shouted "From today, no one will worship Vishnu. I am the God now. Those who will pray or worship Vishnu will be severely punished. From now on, nobody will chant 'Om Namo Narayanaye Namo Ha' but instead chant 'Om Hiranyaye Namo Ha' and this is my order!". Saying this Hiranyakashipu laughed loudly. Back there, Prahlad had gone to gurukul (schools in back days where princes and children used to study). Prahlad had grown into a handsome and very intelligent boy who was around 5-6 years old. He was a great devotee of Lord Vishnu much unlike his dad. Hiranyakashipu hated Vishnu but his son was such a great devotee of Lord Vishnu that Vishnu kept a watch on Prahlad all the time.

Vishnu always smiled when Prahlad sang Vishnu's song and chanted 'Om Namo Narayanaye Namo Ha'. One bright sunny day, Prahlad sat on a rock and was going on chanting 'Om Namo Narayanaye Namo Ha' when his friends, the other students of the gurukul came to the spot. One boy said, "Hey, looks as if Prince Prahlad does not know that he should not chant this mantra". Another said, "Yes. We have to stop him, otherwise if King Hiranyakashipu hears this, young Prahald will get a very severe punishment". The two of them picked two sticks and poked Prahlad in his ears. But nothing could separate Prahlad from his devotion. He kept on chanting 'Om Namo Narayanaye Namo Ha'.

Behind the huts, both the gurus (sages who teach children) talked with each other. One said to the other "Brother Sandh, Prince Prahlad does not know the result of this. King Hiranyakashipu will kill both of us as he will think that we both taught Prahlad to chant this mantra!". Guru Sandh said "Brother, stop him." The Guru shouted "Prahlad!". Both the gurus went towards Prahlad and the other students". Prahlad got up from his seat and greeted his gurus. The gurus said to the other children "You foolish students, don't even know how to greet teachers. Learn something from Prahlad". One boy said "What will we learn? To chant 'Om Namo Narayanaye Namo Ha' and then get killed by Prahlad's father?". Guru Sandh twisted the boy's ear. Prahlad smiled and said "Friends, when we meet our Gurus, we should greet them like this". Saying so, Prahlad joined his palms and said "Namaskar". Soon, all the children joined their palms and said "Namaskar, Namaskar, Namaskar, Namaskar, Namaskar, Namaskar, Namaskar".

Sandh got irritated and said, "Enough. My blessings are with all of you". The children stopped creating a chaos. Both the gurus sat on the rock and said "Prahlad, you should not chant this mantra, 'Om Namo Narayanaye Namo Ha'". Prahlad said, "But we should chant this". Guru Amarkh said, "Listen, Prahlad, now your father, King Hiranyakashipu has conquered the whole world. And the one who is the most powerful should be respected the most. So, you should chant 'Om Hiranyaye Namo Ha'". Prahlad said, "Yes, I agree with this but Lord Vishnu is the Supreme. He is the One and All. 'Om Namo Narayanaye Namo Ha'".

Both the gurus went away to take a bath in anger. Prahlad thought "My gurus are angry with me. They went away because of me. What shall I do now?". The children said, "Prahlad, let's go to play". Prahlad said, "No. Now is the time for chanting and praying". Some children said, "We don't care. We are going to play!". Saying so they ran away but some children stayed back with Prahlad. Prahlad smiled and sang one song of Lord Vishnu which he sang all the time, 'Narayana Narayana hari din dayala Narayana' and the children joined their palms and danced around Prahlad. After some time Hiranyakashipu's army's commander-in-chief came to that place and said "Guru Sandh, Guru Amarkh, King Hiranyakashipu wants you both and Prahlad now in his palace". Sandh asked fearfully "But why?". The chief said, "The king wants to know how his son has studied in the gurukul". Sandh and Amarkh went with Prahlad to Hiranyakashipu's palace with great fear.

5. HIRANYAKASHIPU PUNISHES PRAHLAD

Prahlad ran to his father and mother and they hugged him. Kayadhu said, "My son, I am seeing you after so many days. You have grown so much!". Hiranyakashipu made Prahlad sit on his lap and said "Son, tell me what you learned at gurukul". Sandh looked at Amarkh and said "Death for us!". Prahlad talked about the Vedas and knowledge. He sang the Saraswati Shruti mantra. Hiranyakashipu was very pleased. Prahlad then sang 'Narayana Narayana hari din dayala Narayana'. Hiranyakashipu pushed Prahlad and he fell. Kayadhu picked up her beloved son and said "Husband, spare him. He is just a child".

Hiranyakashipu shouted, "Sandh, Amarkh did you teach my son to chant this? How dare you!". Prahlad moved closer to his father and said "It's not their fault, Dad. They told me many times not to chant this but I chant". Hiranyakashipu grew angry and shook Prahlad hard "Then why are you chanting this?". Prahlad said, "Because Lord Vishnu is the God". Hiranyakashipu punished Prahlad severely. Hiranyakashipu locked Prahlad in a dark cave, tried to burn his hands, pushed him among scorpions and snakes, and kept him in front of giant elephants so that, the elephants would trample over him. But nothing could separate Prahlad from Lord Vishnu. Each time he sang 'Narayana Narayana hari din dayala Narayana' and got saved as Vishnu was saving his dear devotee. Fed up, Hiranyakashipu approached his sister.

6. HOLIKA OFFERS TO HELP

Hiranyakashipu went to his sister, Holika. Holika had a magical blanket which she had got in a boon from a god. The blanket could protect the person wearing it from fire. Hiranyakashipu said, "Sister, can you help me?". Holika said, "Command me, Elder brother". Hiranyakashipu said, "Holika, you have to kill my son, Prahlad. You will sit on the fire flames with Prahlad with your blanket around you. You will be saved but Prahlad will die". That night Hiranyakashipu and Kayadhu watched from the window of their bedroom as Holika sat on the pyre with Prahlad.

Kayadhu cried and fell on the bed when she saw the fire flames. One soldier put the fire on the pyre and Holika laughed out loudly with the blanket around her. Prahlad prayed to Lord Vishnu and to everyone's amazement, the magical blanket flew from Holika and got wrapped around Prahlad. Holika cried "Save me, brother!". But Hiranyakashipu could not do anything. Holika got burned as Hiranyakashipu watched helplessly with tears in his eyes. Prahlad came out fully protected and said to Kayadhu "Mother, Shri Hari saved me". Kayadhu hugged Prahlad. But Hiranyakashipu was boiling with rage.

7. NARASIMHA KILLS HIRANYAKASHIPU

The next morning, Hiranyakashipu, in his royal court stormed towards Prahlad with his mace. Kayadhu stopped him but Hiranyakashipu pushed her and Kayadhu fell hard on the stairs. Prahlad was very scared and cried "Mother!". Hiranyakashipu shouted, "Today, I will kill you Prahlad, and let me see who comes to save you today. Tell me my son, where is your Vishnu?". Prahlad smiled "He is everywhere. In you, in me. In all, everywhere". Hiranyakashipu said, "Oh, is that so? So you mean that he is in this pillar too?".

Hiranyakashipu pointed to a big pillar of the royal court. Prahlad replied "Yes". Hiranyakashipu said, "Then first let me kill your Vishnu before you and then I will kill you". Saying so, he gave a big blow from his mace to the pillar. The pillar started shaking very hardly and all the things, chairs and tables in the royal court fell down. The loud roaring sound of a lion was heard. All the ministers and Asuras ran away fearfully. Now only, Prahlad, Hiranyakashipu, and Kaydhu on the stairs were in the royal court. The pillar broke in a loud clash and came out a creature. Hiranyakashipu veins trembled when he looked at the creature. The creature had a lion face but a man's body and looked extremely angry with his long nails.

Prahlad was scared but then bowed before the 4th incarnation of Lord Vishnu, Shree Narasimha's avatar. Hiranyakashipu tried to hurt Narasimha with his mace but Narasimha carried Hiranyakashipu to the palace's place where it was neither outside nor inside, which means the backyard. Prahlad said "Father, today Shree Narasimha will kill you. As per your boon from Lord Brahma, now it is not day not night, it is afternoon. You are not inside not outside, you are in the backyard. Narasimha will not kill you on Earth or in the sky, he will keep you on his lap and kill you. Shree Narasimha is not a god or an animal or a man, he has an animal's head (lion's head) and a man's body, and finally, Shree Narasimha will not kill you with any weapons. He will kill you with his nails". Hiranyakashipu was very scared.

Shree Narasimha placed Hiranyakashipu on his lap. Narasimha teared off Hiranyakashipu's stomach with his sharp nails and Hiranyakashipu shouted in pain. He died within a short time. After killing Hiranyakashipu, Shree Narasimha was very angry. The gods including Indra Dev came and sang Lord Vishnu's prayer. Prahlad sang 'Narayana Narayana hari din dayala Narayana' and Narasimha came in Lord Vishnu's actual form. All the gods and Prahlad bowed. So, this was how Lord Vishnu killed Hiranyakashipu in the Narasimha avatar. Lord Vishnu looked at Prahlad and smiled.

Test Your Knowledge

Q1. Who was Hiranyakashipu's wife?

a. Indrani
b. A poor girl
c. Kayadhu
d. A demoness

Q2. What did Narada name the child?

a. Prahlad
b. Dhruva
c. Sanatan
d. Hiranyaksha

Q3. What did Holika have?

a. A box
b. A magical blanket
c. A towel
d. A hat

Q4. How did Narasimha avatar look?

a. A normal person
b. Exactly like Lord Vishnu
c. Like a lion
d. His head was like a lion's and his body was like a normal person's body

Q5. Where did Kayadhu fall before being pushed by Hiranyakashipu?

a. On the stairs
b. On her bed
c. On a chair
d. In a pond

5

Vamana Avatar

1. INTRODUCTION

The mother of Indra and the devas, Aditi, sage Kashyap's wife was sad. Bali, king of the Asuras had defeated the gods and conquered heaven. Indra and the gods were roaming here and there for shelter, eating whatever they found, sleeping wherever they saw. Sage Kashyap advised Aditi to pray and please Lord Vishnu and ask him to help the gods. Aditi prayed and meditated following all the rules. S,oon, Vishnu was pleased and he came before Aditi. Aditi touched Vishnu's feet and said "Lord I am so happy to have met you".

Vishnu said, "Devi Aditi, you have pleased me. Ask what you want". Aditi said, "Lord, Bali, king of the asuras has overthrown Indra and the gods. How can a mother see her sons roaming here and there?". Vishnu said, "I understand a mother's pain, Aditi. I will help your sons to regain heaven again. This is my promise". Aditi smiled. Lord Vishnu continued "You will my mother. I will be your son and help the gods regain heaven again". Tears rolled Aditi's eyes. She said, "Lord, you are so kind. You gave me so much more than I wished for. I am so happy to have you as my son". Lord Vishnu smiled and vanished.

2. VAMANA TAKES BIRTH

Aditi closed her eyes. A very shining ray of light was coming from the front. When she opened her eyes, she saw a Brahmin child dressed in white holding a straw umbrella. Aditi knew it was her son, it was Vishnu. Lord Vishnu had taken birth as Vamana. Aditi hugged her son. Vamana said "Mother". Tears rolled down Aditi's cheeks. Aditi said, "Son, you have made your mother so happy". Lord Brahma named the child. He was named Vamana. Aditi said to the 5th incarnation of Lord Vishnu, Vamana avatar "Son, I am blessed to have you as my child". Vamana smiled. He went away walking as Aditi watched him with hope.

3. BALI'S ASHWAMEDH YAGNA

King Bali was organizing Ashwamedh yagna (a yagna which very powerful kings do after defeating almost everyone). Some rishis and guru Shukracharya(guru of the asuras) were seated around the holy fire. They were doing the yagna while Bali was distributing clothes and jewellery to many Brahmins. Bali was very generous. Whoever came to him did not leave empty-handed. He gave anything to anyone who wished for it. He was also a devotee of Lord Vishnu. Bali saw a Brahmin coming towards him. He wore white robes, carried a straw-stick umbrella, and had a pleasant smile on his face.

It was Vamana. Vamana reached near Bali reciting vedas. Bali greeted Vamana "O Holy One, you are a wise brahmin of great knowledge! Kindly introduce yourself. What is your name?". Vamana smiled "Great king Bali, all the names of the world are mine. Now, you only tell me, which name of mine should I tell you?". Shukracharya suddenly paid attention. He had a feeling that this Brahmin was not a normal person. Shukracharya paid attention to what Vamana said. Bali smiled and said, "Then kindly tell me where you live?". Vamana said, "King, a Brahmin does not have a fixed house. Wherever his feet touch the ground, that place becomes his home". Shukracharya using his powers saw Vishnu in Vamana but Bali could not see. Shukracharya sensed that Vishnu had come in Vamana's avatar to destroy the kingdom of Asuras. Bali was mesmerized and pleased with the Brahmin.

4. VAMANA ASKS TO BALI

Bali asked, "Revered sage, you are one of the wisest. Tell me holy one, what help can I be to you?". Vamana said, "I have heard that you give anything to anyone who asks for it. What can you give me?". Bali said, "I can give you wealth, gems, diamonds, precious jewels, a large quantity of food, and many clothes". Vamana smiled "These are all worldly things. What will a Brahmin do with all this? Can you give me what I want?". Bali said, "Ask, holy sage". Vamana said, "I want only as much of land as my three steps can measure. Can you give me?".

Bali stood amazed. He asked, "Revered sage, you want only this much? Are you sure you don't want anything more?". Vamana said, "Those who don't want only as much of land that their 3 steps can measure are never satisfied". Bali went to the holy fire ritual place and brought the holy pot (container where holy water is kept). Vamana raised his hand. Bali was just about to pour the water into the hands of Vamana to make a promise that he would give what Vamana wished for when Shukracharya intervened. He said, "Bali, I can tell you without a doubt that this Brahmin is none other than Lord Vishnu". Bali looked at Vamana confused. He said, "Guru, how can he be Shree Vishnu?". Shukracharya said, "He is Bali. Don't give him land or the asura kingdom will perish. You will lose the kingship of the three worlds". Bali smiled "Guru, even if he is Lord Vishnu, I cannot refuse him.

Imagine the preserver of the world whom everyone prays and worships is standing before me with folded hands. He is asking me for something. I cannot refuse him, guru". Then turning towards Vamana, Bali said, "Sorry for the delay". Shukracharya thought 'I am the guru of the asuras. I have to stop Bali by any means. Thinking so, Shukracharya became very small and got inside the holy water container. When Bali tried to pour water into Vamana's hand, the water did not come out. Bali said, "Sorry, Rishi. Looks like there's an obstacle in the container. Let me fix it". Vamana said, "Don't worry King. Give it to me. I will remove the thing stopping the water". Bali smiled and held the container while Vamana put a small straw inside. The straw poked one of Shukracharya's eyes.

He came out in anger and said with his wounded eye "Bali, being the guru of the asuras, I said for your well-being. I told you not to give this brahmin but you paid no attention. I curse, you will lose your kingdom, and always the asuras will be defeated by the gods. The gods will be superior always". Saying this, Shukracharya went away.

5. BALI BECOMES THE KING OF PATAL LOK

Bali turned towards Vamana and said, "Now I care for nothing as now I will be able to fulfill my promise wholeheartedly". Bali poured the water into Vamana's hand and said to Vamana "I, Bali promise that I will give as much land as your three steps can measure". Vamana smiled and then grew big. Bali and everyone present there stood in amazement as Vamana grew so big that he stood on Earth. The gods and Indra gathered and bowed before Vamana. Bali watched smiling as Vamana kept one foot on Earth and the other on the whole universe. Then Vamana asked, "King Bali, I have kept my first foot on Earth and the second on the whole universe. Where will I put my third step?". Bali smiled "Lord, you have taken everything from me. Now, I have nothing to offer you. But I have to keep my promise so kindly put your third step on my head.

Vamana smiled and descended one foot. All the servants and rishis around Bali ran away in fear. But Bali bowed and Vamana put his foot on Bali's head. Due to force, Bali plunged deeper into the ground and landed on Patal Lok where big mountains and lava reside. Vamana came to Patal Lok and appeared in his original form (Lord Vishnu) before Bali. Vamana said, "Bali, I am very pleased with your charity and devotion towards your promises. Therefore, I announce you as the ruler of Patal Lok. You will rule here truthfully, Bali". Bali bowed before Vamana. Vamana disappeared and went away. This was the story of Vamana avatar of Lord Vishnu.

36

Test Your Knowledge

Q1. Who was the mother of Indra?

a. Aditi
b. Diti
c. Durga maa
d. Kali maa

Q2. Who was the guru of the asuras?

a. Shukracharya
b. Lord Brahma
c. Indra Dev
d. Bali

Q3. What personality did Bali have?

a. Cruelness
b. Generosity
c. Informative
d. Obedient

Q4. What part of Shukracharya's body did the straw damage?

a. Ears
b. Nose
c. One Eye
d. A toe

Q5. What did Bali become at the end?

a. King of heaven
b. King of Patal Lok
c. Ruler of the whole world
d. An ascetic

6

Parshuram Avatar

1. INTRODUCTION

Kartavirya Arjun was a wicked and cruel king of a kingdom. He had a thousand arms. He was so cruel that he insulted and troubled his ministers, soldiers, and servants. Once, he was talking with his wives, when three of his servants came with fruits and water. One servant said, "King, your meal is ready". Kartavirya was disturbed and he said, "Servants, this is not the right time to come. Don't you know this? You disturbed me and therefore you will be severely punished". Saying so, Kartavirya Arjun beat and slapped the three servants. The servants fell down. Arjun laughed and laughed.

Back there, Rishi Jamdagni and his wife Renuka had 5 sons. Their names were Rumanvan, Suhotra, Vasu and Visvavasu. The 5th and youngest one was named Ram. He was very powerful and had mastered fighting. Lord Shiva taught Ram. Shiva personally taught him and made him master many weapons.

2. RAM GETS ANOTHER NAME

One morning, Lord Shiva was teaching Ram with a spear in a forest. Ram aimed and threw the spear with great speed. Shiva was very pleased. Ram turned back and saw Shiva sitting on a rock holding his Trishul (Lord Shiva's weapon). Ram touched Shiva's feet. Shiva smiled "Ram, I am very pleased with your skills. Today I will give you that weapon which nobody has or has ever used".

Lord Shiva raised his hand and a weapon which was sharp on both sides appeared on Shiva's hand. Shiva gave that to Ram and said "Ram, this weapon is called Parshu. This weapon will be your identity. From today, you will be known as Parshuram". Ram said, "Guru, I am so thankful to you for this wonderful gift". Saying so, Parshuram returned to Jamdagni's ashram.

3. PARSHURAM CUTS HIS MOTHER RENUKA'S HEAD

One day, rishi Jamdagni was performing a ritual. Parshuram had gone out somewhere. Jamdagni sent Renuka to bring some water for the ritual from a river. Renuka was so faithful to her husband, rishi Jamdagni, that the pot in which she filled water was made from soft clay. But that day, something else happened. While Renuka was filling her pot, she saw one Gandharva (heavenly being 'men') bathing in the river with his three wives. They splashed in the water, thoroughly enjoying themselves.

Renuka thought 'How lucky that ladies are!'. Renuka filled her pot and stood up. She gazed at the handsome Gandharva and thought 'How they are enjoying! If ever I could enjoy a moment like this. But I am just imagining things. Thinking all this, Renuka was completely unfocused and the clay pot fell from her hands and broke into pieces spilling all the water. Renuka said, "Oh no! What happened? This has never happened before. Now what will I tell my husband?". Back there in the ashram, Jamdagni was waiting for Renuka and when she did not even come back after a long time, Jamdagni said "Sons, where did your mother go?". Vasu said, "Let me go and see". Jamdagni said, "You don't need to go, Vasu. I will see using my powers".

Jamdagni used his powers and saw where was Renuka. He witnessed all the things that had happened. After seeing all that, Jamdagni shouted "Renuka!". The shout was so loud that Renuka heard it from the river. She rushed to the ashram. Jamdagni said, "Renuka, I know what has happened. How could you betray me?". Renuka sobbed "Husband, forgive me. It's not my fault. It was a mistake". Jamdagni shouted, "Enough! I know everything Renuka". Then turning towards his sons, Jamdagni said "My sons, your mother has lost her purity. Kill Renuka!". Renuka was shocked. The four sons present there were surprised. They asked, "Father, how can we kill a woman? How can we kill our mother? It is written in the Vedas that killing a mother is a sin".

Jamdagni replied angrily "But it is also written that not obeying father is a sin". The four sons stood with folded hands. Jamdagni said, "Are you four teaching me the Vedas? You are not listening to me after I order also? I curse you Rumanvan, Suhotra, Vasu, and Visvavasu that you will become statues this moment". Saying so, Jamdagni sprinkled water on his sons. They instantly turned into statues. Renuka cried and shouted, "Husband Jamdagni, why did you punish my sons? I had to get the punishment. Why did you make my children suffer?". As Renuka sobbed Parshuram entered the ashram and saw his brother's statues, mother crying and father standing angrily. Parshuram asked, "What happened, father?". Jamdagni replied, "Son, your mother Renuka has lost her purity. Kill her". Parshuram raised his Parshu and instantly cut Renuka's head without a thought. The body and head of Renuka fell to the ground.

For once, Jamdagni could not understand anything. He said, "Parshuram, I asked you to kill Renuka in anger but you killed her?". Parshuram smiled

"Father, obeying your command is my highest duty". Jamdagni said, "Son, you are very wise. Ask whatever you wish for. Parshuram said without a doubt "Father, using your powers, please make my mom alive again and turn my brothers into their actual form". Jamdagni smiled and did what Parshuram said. Renuka was so happy to see her sons alive. Parshuram asked for forgiveness but Renuka said "Son, this act of yours will be followed by generations to come. It will be an example of Pitrudharm (son's duty towards his father or mother)". Parshuram hugged his mother and they stayed happily for some days.

4. JAMDAGNI IS KILLED

One day, while Parshuram had gone out to bring wood, Kartavirya Arjun entered Rishi Jamdagni's ashram and demanded food for him and his army. Renuka, Jamdagni, and their four sons went away. Actually Kamadhenu (the wish fulling cow) was gifted to rishi Jamdagni from the gods. Jamdagni and Renuka along with their four sons prayed to the holy cow and the cow produced many delicious dishes on a table. Kartavirya had been observing all these. He went to Jamdagni and said, "Rishi, this cow should not belong to a hermit. It can give me what I wish for. Give me this cow". Kartavirya laughed loudly. Jamdagni said, "The gods have gifted this cow to me. I can't give you this holy cow". Kartavirya killed Jamdagni and his four sons and dragged away Kamdhenu forcefully as Renuka watched helplessly.

When Parshuram returned, he saw the dead bodies of his brothers and father. He saw his mother Renuka crying bitterly near Jamdagni's dead body. Renuka narrated the events which took place as Parshuram hugged his mother and cried. But then Parshuram stood up and said "Today, I Parshuram son of Rishi Jamdagni, take a vow that I will kill Kartavirya Arjun and his sons and keep on killing cruel kings as many times my dad and brothers were stabbed". Then, Parshuram stormed off to Kartavirya's palace with his Parshu.

5. PARSHURAM KILLS KARTAVIRYA ARJUN

Parshuram killed the soldiers as he entered the royal court. Kartavirya Arjun, seeing Parshuram said, "You rishi Putra (son of a sage), how did you get inside my palace. Wait, I will kill you and send you near to your father and brother". Parshuram asked, "Why did you kill my dad and brothers? Just for Kamdhenu?". Kartavirya said, "If they had not stopped me I would not have killed them. I am the king of this kingdom. Everything here belongs to me". Parshuram said, "So, my dad's and brothers' lives also belong to you?".

Kartavirya ordered his sons and soldiers present there to kill Parshuram but Parshuram killed all of them. Kartavirya said, "Why did you kill my sons? Wait, I will kill you". Kartavirya stormed towards Parshuram with two maces. Parshuram cut Kartavirya's hands but two more hands appeared because Kartavirya had a thousand arms. The more Parshuram cut Kartavirya's hands, the more hands appeared. Finally, Parshuram cut Kartavirya's head and he fell dead. It was believed to avenge the murder of his father by a Kshatriya, he killed all the male Kshatriyas on earth 21 successive times. This was the story of the 6th incarnation of Lord Vishnu, Shree Parshuram Avatar.

Test Your Knowledge

Q1. How many hands did Kartavirya Arjun have?

a. 2
b. 1000
c. 100
d. 10000

Q2. What was the name of the weapon which Lord Shiva gave to Parshuram?

a. Vajra
b. Trishul
c. Sudarshan Chakra
d. Parshu

Q3. How many sons did rishi Jamadagni have?

a. 10
b. 5
c. 7
d. 4

Q4. What did rishi Jamadagni curse his 4 sons?

a. to become statues
b. to drown in water
c. to become ash
d. to die that very moment

Q5. Kamadhenu was which animal?

a. Tiger
b. Lion
c. Cow
d. Elephant

7
Ram Avatar

1. INTRODUCTION

Ravan was an asura king who ruled over Lanka which was surrounded by oceans and seas. He was very cruel king. Ravan was a Brahmin and a great devotee of Lord Shiva. The gods were also powerless before Ravan. The gods went to Vaikuntha and told Lord Vishnu about Ravan. Brahma said, "Vishnu, it's time for your 7th incarnation". Vishnu smiled.

At that time King Dasharath, a very wise, and good king ruled over Ayodhya, a very prosperous city. Dasharath had 3 wives. The eldest one was Kaushalya, the middle one was Kaikei, and the younger one was Sumitra. King Dasharath did a yagna and Agni Dev gave Dasharath a bowl of kheer (pudding made with rice) to distribute among his wives to give birth to sons. Kaushalya and Kaikei ate one spoon while they made Sumitra eat two spoons.

2. RAM IS BORN

In the meantime, the 3 queens gave birth to 4 sons and Dasharath beamed with pride. Sage Vashistha, the kulguru (main sage of a city or kingdom in the olden days) of Ayodhya named Kaushalya's son, Ram (who was actually Vishnu- 7th incarnation), Kaikei's son, Bharat and Sumitra's sons, Lakshman and Shatrughan. Ram was the eldest followed by Bharat, Lakshman, and the smallest, Shatrughan. The four princes grew up with love and care from their mothers and father.

When they were of suitable age to go to gurukul (schools in olden times), Sage Vashistha took them to his ashram and taught them warfare, Vedas, knowledge, and many other things. Many other princes and children went to study there. Ram became a very experienced fighter and he was also very compassionate and kind. Everyone loved Ram dearly due to his good attitude. Lakshman treated Ram very well and took care of his elder brother. He was very devoted to Ram. When the four princes finished their learnings, Vashistha took them back to Ayodhya where their mothers and father welcomed them with open hands.

3. GOING WITH VISHWAMITRA

The four princes had grown into young and handsome boys. After a few days, Sage Vishwamitra came and asked Dasharath to send Ram with him to kill the demons disturbing their yagnas. Dasharath loving Ram the most, thought that Ram would be injured and tried to persuade Vishwamitra. But Vishwamitra was still and just on his statement and finally, Dasharath sent Ram along with Lakshman as Lakshman never wanted to get separated from Ram.

On their way to Vishwamitra's ashram with Vishwamita, Ram killed the demoness Tadka. Vishwamita took both the princes to his ashram and Ram and Lakshman killed all the demons who tried to disturb Vishwamitra's yagna. Vishwamitra was very pleased and gave Ram many divine weapons.

4. SITA SWAYAMVAR

That time King Janak, king of Mithila, held a swayamvara (where princesses chose princes or princes had to do a certain work to marry the princess) for his daughter Sita. Janak had found Sita as a baby while ploughing the field. Sunayana was Janak's wife and Kushadhvaja was his younger brother. Sita and Urmilla were Janak's daughters while Mandvi and Shutakirti were Kushadhvaja's daughters. Vishwamitra was also invited to the Swayamvar. He took Ram and Lakshman along with him. On their way, Ram helped Ahalya, a woman sage to become her actual form from a stone by a curse by her husband, Rishi Gautam.

When the 3 people reached Mithila, they were welcomed by Janak. Janak was very pleased to know that the sons of Dasharath, Ram, and Laksman had also come to attend the Swayamvar. Janak had got Lord Shiva's bow in a boon. The Swayamvar's rules were that the one who would string that bow would marry Sita. While all the princes and kings failed to do so, Ram easily broke the bow and married Sita. Sita was very beautiful and Dasharath came instantly with Vashistha, Bharat, and Shatrughan to Mithila to attend the marriage of his eldest son. When Dasharath talked with Janak, they decided that Ram would marry Sita, Bharat would marry Mandvi, Lakshman would marry Urmilla and Shatrughan would marry Shutakirti. The 4 princes married the 4 princesses and they came back to Ayodhya after the princesses bid farewell to their family. Kaushalya, Kaikei, and Sumitra welcomed their sons and their brides and for some days the large family lived happily.

5. 14 YEARS IN EXILE

Dasharath was very happy to see his sons happy with their wives. Dasharath specially instructed Kaushalya to take good care of the young brides as he had promised to Janak. Day by day Dasharath grew old. He noticed that Ram cared for him very much. He also noticed that everyone in Ayodhya adored him for his good attitude and respect towards others. So, he decided to make Ram the Yuvraj (the heir). He sat with his ministers and advisors and told them about his decision. Everyone agreed readily and it was decided that the crowning of Ram as the heir would be done on a auspicious day. Kaushalya, Sumitra, Kaikei, Bharat, Satrughan, Lakshman, Ram and Sita were very happy. That time, Bharat's uncle became very sick. So, one messenger came and took Bharat and Satrughan to their uncle's palace.

The day before the day of the crowning of Ram was celebrated enthusiastically. Big drums were played and people sang and danced on the streets of Ayodhya. That night, Manthara, the maid of Kaikei was bursting with anger. She rushed to Kaikei and shouted, "Queen, Ram is going to be crowned tomorrow!". Kaikei said, "Yes, I am very happy. Here, take this this necklace is for you". Manthara threw the necklace on the ground and said "The thing which surprises me is how you are so happy with this. Ram will be the heir and Bharat nothing! Ram will treat Bharat as his slave and Kaushalya will treat you as her maid". Kaikei shouted, "Never! Have you gone mad, Manthara? My son, Ram will never be so rude to me". But Manthara kept on arguing and soon a wave of hatred for Ram rose in Kaikei's mind. Manthara said, "You have to stop Ram from being the heir".

Kaikei said, "But how can I do this is this night only? I have only a very few hours left". Manthara whispered, "Did you forget the boons, king Dasharath gave you?". Kaikei smiled "Yes, many years ago King Dasharath and I had joined Indra's forces to defeat the demons. In the war, a spear struck King Dasharath in his chest and he fell wounded. I rode the chariot and brought back King Dasharath to Ayodhya safely. He was very pleased with me and he asked me to ask for any two boons. I had refused but said that I would use them when needed. But what will I ask him?". Manthara said, "The first boon will be that Bharat will be the king in place of Ram and the second boon you will ask will be that Ram will go to the jungle for 14 years". Kaikei agreed. Kaikei went to Dasharath's room and asked him for the two boons. Dasharath's heart melted when Kaikei spoke those words.

But Dasharath had to keep his promise, no matter what. Dasharath cried and cried and even fell at Kaikei's feet but she was adamant.

The next morning Arya Sumant, one of the main ministers was organising the grand ceremony. He was searching for Dasharath but he could not find him anywhere. Arya Sumant went to Dasharath's room and found him sad and wiping tears. He was surprised but before he could ask, Kaikei said "Go and bring Ram here immediately!". Arya Sumant rushed to Ram's palace. Ram was helping Sita to tie her long, black hair. Arya Sumant asked Ram to come with him to Dasharath's palace. Ram went with Arya Sumant to Dasharath. On the way, all the people of Ayodhya and the ministers asked Arya Sumant about Dasharath. Arya Sumant said there was an emergency and Ram and Arya rode quickly on a chariot towards Dasharath's palace.

When they reached, Ram found Dasharath in tears. Kaikei said, "Ram, long ago, your dear father, Dasharath had gone to fight the demons to help Indra..........". Kaikei explained everything to Ram. She also told Ram that she had asked the 2 boons and told him what she had asked. Kaikei said, "So, your father is wiping tears because you will have to go away". Dasharath cried "Oh my Ram, don't leave me. Kaikei betrayed me! She is a very bad mother. Don't go away". Kind Ram said "No father. Queen Kaikei is my mother after all. Don't worry father. I am so happy that I will go to the forest fulfilling the boons you had given to mother Kaikei. I will also have the company of so many sages in the forests. Allow me Father".

Ram went to Kaushalya and told her what had happened. Kaushalya said, "Kaikei! How could she punish my son like this?". Ram replied, "Calm down Mother. I will go!". When Ram told Sita to stay in Ayodhya till he returned after 14 years, Sita refused and said wherever Ram go, she would follow him. When Ram informed Lakshman, he insisted, he would go too as he could not live without his dear elder brother. So with Lakshman and Sita, Ram went to Dasharath. Kaikei exclaimed, "Why are you still wearing royal garments? Change into the dresses of ascetics immediately!". Lakshman was bursting with rage but Ram smiled and changed his dress. Manthara helped Sita to wear an ascetic's saree. Vashistha told Sita to wear the jewellery still. Dasharath cried and cried. Ram, Lakshman, and Sita took everyone's blessings and went away.

They packed a few ascetic clothes and Arya Sumant took Ram, Sita, and Lakshman in a royal chariot to the outskirts of Ayodhya. When they reached the border of Ayodhya, Ram got out and wrapped some soil in a piece of cloth and said "I will always worship this sacred soil of Ayodhya". A new kingdom came called Kevati. Ram shouted, "What! This is Kevati? And Nishadraj is the king of this kingdom, Arya Sumant? Nishad is my friend!". Ram, Lakshman, and Sita sat under a banyan tree and waited for Nishadraj. Arya Sumant brought Nishadraj. Nishadraj fell at Ram's feet and Ram hugged him tightly. Nishadraj said, "I know that Queen Kaikei had told you to go into exile for 14 years. Friend, please stay in my kingdom for those 14 years".

Ram said, "I cannot, I have to stay in deep forests". The next day, Ram and Lakshman matted their hair. Ram, Lakshman, and Sita bid farewell to Nishad and went to a river. A boatman offered to give the three of them a free ride across the river. Arya Sumant told Ram that he would accompany them but Ram politely refused and said Arya to go back to Ayodhya and take care of Dasharath. So, Arya Sumant went back when Ram, Lakshman, and Sita crossed the river. After that, the three of them crossed many rivers, dense forests, and ashrams. As suggested by many rishis and sages, Ram, Lakshman, and Sita made a hut of mud and straw in Chitrakoot. There was a small pond and trees laden with fruits outside their house. For many days the three of them lived happily.

6. DEATH OF DASHARATH

Back in Ayodhya, Dasharath missed Ram terribly and when Arya Sumant informed him that he had left them near a river, he was heartbroken. Soon he became very sick and unhealthy. Dasharath was not able to even walk out of his room. Kaikei did not talk to him much. Kaushalya and Sumitra were always at Dasharath's side in his room. Dasharath was already very old and the separation from his dear son made his situation worse. Finally crying and weeping for Ram, Dasharath breathed his last. While dying, he said to Kaushalya and Sumitra "Wives, my death time has come. Before dying, I shall tell you the reason for my death.

Long, long ago, when I was a young prince, I loved hunting at night very much. I was also a skilled archer. One night, I was hunting near a river when I heard the sound of gurgling of water. I shot an arrow, thinking it to be an animal. But, actually, it was Shravana Kumar. He was a young man whose parents were blind. His parents were thirsty, so, he had come to fetch water for them. Shravana was very much devoted to his parents and took care of their every need. When I went to the spot, I saw Shravana lying in pain with the arrow struck in his chest. I immediately ran to him and apologized and asked him that whatever punishment he would give me, I would accept it. He was very kind-hearted so he asked me to just fetch water in the pot and give it to his parents. With these last words, he died.

I went to his parents in the deep/dark night and made his father first drink the water. His father said, "You are not our son. I don't feel that you are Shravana. Tell me who are you?". I with tears explained everything. Hearing what had happened to her son, Shravana's mother died instantly/on the spot. His father got very angry and cursed me that I would die when my son parted with me. Shravana's father also died". Saying these words Dasharath closed his eyes. Kaushalya and Sumitra's loud weeping sound alerted everyone and they came rushing. Even Kaikei was crestfallen. Vashistha kept the dead body of Dasharath in a big tub of oil. In the old days, a son performed the last rites of his father. Arya Sumant and the ministers decided to send for Bharat immediately. Some soldiers and ministers went to Bharat's uncle and brought Bharat and Shatrughan back to Ayodhya. Manthara stood in front of the door in which Dasharath was lying.

When Bharat and Shatrughan approached worriedly, Manthara stopped them by saying "King has gone somewhere, you go to your mother". Bharat went to Kaikei. Bharat touched her feet and she served him fresh fruits and water. Bharat asked "Where is father? When I entered the palace all the people of Ayodhya were staring at me as if they were cursing me in their minds. Has something occurred in my absence of presence? Tell me, mother, tell me". Kaikei smiled and described everything - Bharat was the king, the exiling of Ram for 14 years, Lakshman and Sita accompanied him, and the death of Dasharath. Bharat shouted "Mother! Why did you do all this? I know that my dear brother Ram would never make me his servant or mother Kaushalya will make you hers. You exiled him for 14 years mother? 14 years? And that fact also that my younger Lakshman also went? Along with my loving sister-in-law, Mata Sita? What harm had they done to you, mother? I would have never liked to be the king when my brothers and sister-in-law would stay and roam in the forest for 14 years.

Why did you do this mother? And father died because of you. Just because you wanted me to become the king, you sent away my brother which led to the death of my father?". Bharat stood up "I am going, mother. And I shall never talk to you again, mother. Never!". Kaikei ran after him but Bharat had made up his mind. Kaikei now realized what mistake she had made. Bharat performed the last rites of Dasharath. Then he decided to go with Vashistha, ministers, and soldiers to Ram to convince him and bring him back to Ayodhya to become the king. Vashistha agreed.

Bharat was sure that Ram would come so when Urmilla expressed her desire to see Lakshman at least once, Bharat said that when Lakshman would come, she would see her every day, every time. So she didn't go. Janak and Sunayana also went. When Kaikei asked Bharat if she could go, Bharat replied "Why, mother? Are 14 years too short? You want to go so that you can tell Ram brother, to stay some more years". Kaikei hung her head in shame. Kaushalya who had been observing all this said "Bharat, Kaikei is your mother after all. You should not behave with her like this. Kaikei will go with all of us and this is my command".

So, Kaushalya, Kaikei and Sumitra went along. They took horses, elephants, and many soldiers. They met Nishadraj who offered to accompany them. There Ram, Sita, and Lakshman had settled in Chitrakoot with some sages. Bharat reached there and Ram hugged him. After welcoming Bharat said that Dasharath had died. Ram and Lakshman cried and hugged each other. Sita was also very sad. They performed the last rites. When Bharat and Vashistha told Ram to go back to Ayodhya with them, he refused saying that I can't disobey my father. The armies put up their tents and lived for a few days. But Ram decided that he wouldn't return. Janak and Vashistha held a meeting to decide what had to be done. Ram said, "I cannot go back to Ayodhya. To fulfill the wish of my father, I have to stay here for more 14 years".

So, it was decided that until the 14 years were over and Ram returned, Bharat would rule over Ayodhya. But Bharat loved Ram very much. He took Ram's slippers and put them on the royal throne of Ayodhya. He wore the dresses of ascetics which Ram also wore and lived in Nandigram, near Ayodhya's palace in a straw hut managing all the works of a king.

Ram, Lakshman, and Sita decided to move to a new place. Ram told the rishis that Bharat loved him very much and he could come again which could disturb their meditations and yagnas so, they would go deep into the Dandaka Aranya forest and look for a new place to stay. So they packed their things and walked to a new place to stay.

7. RAVAN ABDUCTS SITA

They walked on for many days and met many rishis. They killed many asuras (demons) on their way. Ram's feet would get brushed and bleed while

Lakshman washed them with cloth and water. They would eat yummy berries that grew on trees. 13 years had passed. Ram, Lakshman, and Sita saw a big, white bird sitting on a rock one day. Ram asked, "Great bird, who are you? Kindly tell me your name and birthplace. I am Ram, the eldest son of King Dasharath of Ayodhya and she is Sita, my wife, and Lakshman, my younger brother". The bird smiled "Ram, you have pleased me by taking the name of my friend, Dasharath. Your father was my friend. I had helped him in many wars. Sage Kashyapa and Vinata had given birth to Garuda and Aruna. Garuda became the vehicle of Lord Vishnu. Aruna became the charioteer of Surya Dev. Aruna had married Shyeni and gave birth to me and my elder brother Sampati. My name is Jatayu. I will always protect you.

You should build a cottage there". Jataya pointed to a place near the rock where he was sitting. Ram said, "We will be happy and safe under your protection". Lakshman built a gate and a big house with mud and straw. Ram was amazed and Sita was very happy. They lived happily for many days. Then one day, Shoorpankha (a demoness who was the younger sister of Ravan) was roaming around the forest. She lived in Janasthan with her brothers Khar and Dooshan. She saw Ram meditating in the cottage and was enchanted by his handsomeness. She did Maya (magic or illusion) and changed her demoness form to a beautiful apsara. She approached Ram and asked, "Who are handsome, man? I have never seen you before. Will you marry me?".

Ram smiled "Beautiful lady, my name is Ram, prince of Ayodhya and the eldest son of King Dasharath. I can't marry you as I have already married. She is my wife, Sita". And he pointed to Sita who was arranging flowers. Ram said "But you can ask my younger brother, Lakshman". Shoorpankha turned to Lakshman who was chopping a bundle of wood for cooking. Lakshman said, "I can't marry you as I am also married. I serve my brother Ram, and think of myself as his slave and a slave has no right to marry anyone". Shoorpankha went to Ram and changed into her real demoness form. She was very angry and said, "Are you rejecting me just because of this girl, Sita? Then wait. I will kill her and then you will be forced to marry me!". She rushed towards Sita and grabbed her. Sita screamed. Lakshman rushed with a sword and cut Shoorpankha's nose. Shoorpankha cried in pain and said, "My brothers, Khar and Dooshan will take revenge, Ram". She flew away. Soon after, Khar and Dooshan lined up with their armies outside Ram's cottage. Ram single-handedly killed all the soldiers along with Khar and Dooshan. The only one who was able to leave alive was Shoorpankha who immediately flew to Lanka where Ravan ruled.

Ram entered the cottage and kept his bow and arrows in the cottage. Shoorpankha entered Ravan's court, crying. Ravan asked, "Shoorpankha, you here? And what happened to your nose? Who dared to hurt you, dear younger sister?". Shoorpankha hid her mistake and lied "Brother, a very handsome prince named Ram has come and is staying for 14 years in the forest in a cottage along with his brother Lakshman and his wife Sita. Sita is very, very beautiful. She looks like a goddess. She isn't suitable to stay with Ram in the dense forest. I thought to bring her to you, but when I went closer to her Lakshman cut my nose. Sita is very beautiful and you should make her your queen".

Ravan said dreamily "Really? Is Sita that beautiful? Then she has no place with that hermit, Ram. I will bring her and make her my wife, the queen of Lanka. Shoorpankha, I will take revenge". Vibhisan, Ravan's younger brother told Ravan that stealing somebody's wife was not the right thing to do and he should not do that and it was Shoorpankha's fault that she disturbed their family's peace. But Ravan was enchanted with Sita's beauty and he had decided to make her his queen. Ravan went to Maricha, his maternal uncle, and told him to help him. Maricha also advised Ravan not to get into a fight with Ram. He said, "Ravan, why do you want to marry Sita when you have your wife Mandodari and many other queens? It is not the right thing to do so". But Ravan said, "Uncle, you are related to me. You are bound to help me. You have to do something". Maricha agreed.

One morning, Ravan and Maricha reached the cottage where Ram, Lakshman, and Sita lived. Ravan hid behind a tree. Maricha took the form of a golden deer and roamed around in front of the cottage. Sita noticed the beautiful deer and requested Ram to bring it to her. Lakshman said, "Bhabi, (sister-in-law in Hindi) I don't think that it is a real golden deer. I think there is some maya (magic or illusion)behind it". But Sita requested Ram and Ram said "Lakshman, I am going to catch the golden deer. You stay here and protect Sita". Saying this, Ram took his bow and arrow and headed towards the deer. Meanwhile, Ravan had been watching all this. Maricha (who had taken the form of the golden deer) ran very deep into the forest with Ram following him.

Maricha took Ram very deep into the forest. When Ram was much away from the cottage, Maricha stopped for a while. Ram shot an arrow at the deer and the deer fell shouting "Lakshman, Sita!" exactly in Ram's voice. Sita said, "Lakshman, that is her husband's voice. I hope he is in some kind of trouble. Go and help him". Lakshman said, "Sister, nobody in this world can harm my brother. Don't worry". But, Sita was too worried and kept arguing and persuading Lakshman to go. When Lakshman didn't go, Sita said "You, don't want to help your elder brother? How did you become such? When did you start to disobey me? Go, and help your brother. Lakshman, go". Lakshman finally agreed and said, "But sister, see". He took out one of his arrows and drew a line on the sand around the cottage. Lakshman said, "Bhabi (sister-in-law in Hindi), this is Lakshman rekha. It is very powerful.

Nobody can enter the cottage when this Rekha is there. You should never go out of the cottage sister unless we are back". Lakshman went away. Ravan peeped out and saw Sita. He thought "Oh my god! Is she really Sita? How beautiful she is! I will surely marry her and take her to Lanka. Whatever Shoorpankha had said was true". When Ravan saw that Lakshman had gone far away, he took the form of a hermit using Maya (magic or illusion) and entered the gate of the cottage.

He asked "Alms (food given to poor people or hermits), give alms". Sita was standing on the border of the cottage. Ravan asked in a kind voice "Daughter, will you please give me some alms?". Sita went in and Ravan tried to enter the cottage but when he tried, something like a spark burned. Ravan immediately understood what was happening and thought of another plan. He sat on a rock. When she came out, Ravan opened his eyes and said "Daughter, I have sat down. Please bring my food here". Sita was shocked.

She remembered Lakshman's warning. She said politely "Holy Sage, kindly come here and take your fruits. There is nobody at home and I can't leave the cottage". Ravan stood up and said, "You dare to disobey me. Then wait, I will curse your husband right away". Sita was scared. She said, "No, no holy sage. Please forgive me". She thought for a while but then holding the plate of fruits, crossed the line and went to Ravan. Ravan smiled wickedly. He changed into his real asura form. Sita threw the plate and ran towards the cottage screaming. But Ravan grabbed her and took her to Puspak Viman (Lord Kuber's vehicle which Ravan had stolen). Ravan flew away with Sita. Sita screamed and screamed but all that was heard in response was just Ravan's laughter.

There, Ram found Lakshman. Ram said, "Lakshman, what you had said was true. The golden deer was an evil man who did maya (magic or illusion) named Maricha. But why did you come here?". Lakshman said, "I and my sister-in-law heard your voice crying for our help. Sister Sita, urged me to come here, so I came". Ram replied "It was not me. It was the golden deer.

As it fell dead, it transformed into its actual human form and cried out your names in my voice. Lakshman, I feel that there is something not right in our cottage". Ram and Lakshman rushed to their cottage and found that Sita was missing.

There Jatayu had heard Sita's screams. He flew up to Puspak Viman and attacked Ravan. But Ravan was very powerful. He cut one of Jatayu's wings who fell extremely wounded. Ram searched along with Lakshman and soon they reached Jatayu who was lying almost dead. Ram rushed to him, held Jatayu's head, and asked "Great bird, you are like my father. Tell me, what happened to you? Who has hurt you?". Jatayu whispered "Ram, the king of Lanka, the demon Ravan has taken away your wife by force to Lanka in the South. When I tried to attack him and help Sita, Ravan cut one of my wings. I am going to die soon. You both go and protect Sita. Head for South". Jatayu died. Ram performed his last rites. Then carrying some food, clothes, bow and arrow, Ram and Lakshman headed towards South.

8. FRIENDSHIP WITH SUGREEVA AND DEATH OF VALI

On their way, Ram killed many demons. Ram killed a demon which turned into a prince/god. He said to walk further and they will meet an old woman, Sabari who has been waiting all her life to meet Ram. Ram and Lakshman walked and walked till they reached Sabari's small hut. Sabari hut put marigold flowers on the street to welcome Ram and Lakshman. Sabari fell at Ram's feet as Ram picked her up. Sabari gave Ram and Lakshman some berries from which she had taken bites. Lakshman hated the berries from the first sight of the berries from which Sabari had taken bites. But Ram ate whole-heartedly much to the delight of Sabari and much to the disgust of Lakshman. Sabari said "Lord, walk a little more then you will reach Rishyamukh mountain. There is Sugreeva who is a vanar (part monkey part human). You go and become his friend. He will surely help you. Now, it's time for me to go". After that, Sabari chanted a mantra and died in a yogic way. Ram and Lakshman again started walking and soon reached Rishyamukh.

There they met Sugreeva, Jambhavan, and Hanumaan. Ram narrated everything and Sugreeva soon said "Lord Ram, from now on we are friends. Promise me that you will help me, and then I will promise you that I will help you to find Mata Sita". Ram said, "But how can I help you". Sugreeva said "Lord, my elder brother Vali and I lived in Kiskindha, a palace and my brother ruled there. Once a demon named Dundubhi who is in the form of a bull but was a demon challenged Vali to fight with him. They fought in a cave. I was guarding the cave's entrance. After some days, I heard a scream in pain voice from inside. Blood came rushing out of the cave like a stream of water. I thought that my elder brother Vali was dead, so I picked up a very large stone and kept it at the entrance of the cave completely closing it. I went back to Kiskindha and declared that Vali was dead. So, they declared me as the king. But actually, Dudunbhi was dead. Vali opened the cave with much effort and threw the bull (Dudunbhi) very far.

The demon fell at Sage Matanga's ashram near Rishyamukh mountain and the ashram was covered with the large bull's blood. Sage Matanga cursed Vali that he wouldn't be able to enter Rishyamukh mountain and if he tried, his head would be broken into 1000 pieces. When Vali returned to Kiskindha and saw me as the king, he beat me very hard. I ran and ran and came here and took shelter. You have to kill him and make me the king again so that we can fight with Ravan with the vanar army". Ram agreed. Hanumaan brought a cloth and gave it to Ram. Ram opened it and found Sita's jewellery. Hanumaan said "Lord, once when we were sitting on a rock. We saw this cloth on the ground. It was the time when Ravan was taking away Mata Sita. She threw this jewellery down from the Puspak Viman. We have kept it". Tears from Ram's eyes rolled.

The next day, Sugreeva went to Kiskindha and told him to fight with him. Vali agreed and they both went to a vast field. Vali and Sugreeva started to fight while Ram, Lakshman, Jambhavan, and Hanumaan hid behind a tree. Ram took out an arrow and aimed it. But Sugreeva and Vali were brothers. They looked exactly like twins. Ram could not understand who was Sugreeva and who was Vali. Vali beat Sugreeva badly and he returned extremely wounded. He said, "Lord Ram, you did not save me. Why?". Ram told Sugreeva the problem and told him to fight again the next day but wear a garland of flowers so he could recognize him. So, the next day Vali and Sugreev fought again, and this time Ram killed Vali. As he lay dying, Vali's wife Tara and his son Angad came running to the spot. They cried bitterly. Sugreeva was also a bit sad. Ram felt pity for Vali and blessed him with a boon. Vali died.

Angad then came to Sugreeva's support. Then, Sugreeva became the king. It was rainy season and Ram decided to start with the army after the rain had completely stopped. So, they waited for the season to end. After the season ended, Ram, Lakshman, and Sugreeva decided to send a small part of their army to go and search for Sita first. Ram who loved Hanumaan dearly expected him to reach Sita so Ram gave his ring to Hanumaan and said "Give this to Sita. She will recognize it as it is mine". Hanumaan leaded the army with Angad and Jambhavan along with Nal and Neel the twin sons of the Ashwini Kumars. They went to the seashore. Jambhavan said "Lanka is on the other side of the sea. But who will swim and reach there? Nobody dared to do the task.

Jambhavan went to Hanumaan who was sitting on a rock in deep thought. Jambhavan said, "Hanumaan, only you can do this great task". Hanumaan stood up amazed "Me, no. I can't swim across the sea to Lanka". Jambhavan said "Hanumaan, when you were young you were very powerful and too naughty. You angered a sage and he cursed you that you would forget all your powers unless somebody would remind you of them. Today I remind you Hanumaan. Remember the past. Go to Lanka. Only you can do it, Hanumaan".

9. HANUMAAN GOES TO LANKA

Hanumaan grew his size. Soon, it seemed as if he touched the sky. He flew away as the vanars cheered. On his way, he came across a demoness whom he killed who instantly changed into a goddess. She explained that she was sent by the gods to test Hanumaan. Hanumaan came across a mountain that was his father's friend and he wanted him to rest on it but Hanumaan said that he was busy. After a long journey, Hanumaan reached Lanka whose gates were guarded by a demoness whom Hanumaan killed. The demoness whose name was Lankeni said "It was destined that when I would be defeated by a monkey, from that day destruction will take place in Lanka".

Hanumaan became very small and began to fly through the Golden City. He saw Ravan sleeping along with Mandodari (Ravan's wife). He saw Vibhisan chanting Ram's name and asked him "Who are you?". Vibhisan said, "I am Vibhisan, a devotee of Lord Ram. I am the younger brother of Ravan. I have told him many times to return Mata Sita to Lord Ram but he never listens to me". Hanumaan said, "My greetings to you. I am Hanumaan, one of Lord Ram's soldier". He flew and finally reached Ashok Vatika where Ravan had kept Sita captive. He decided to meet Sita. He went to Sita and bowed before her. Sita stood up scared "Who are you?". Hanumaan said, "Don't be scared, Mata Sita. I am Hanumaan, a vanar. I am Lord Ram's devotee and one of the vanar army". He gave the ring to Sita. Tears rolled down her cheeks. She said, "Hanumaan, you have pleased me. Thank you so much. Does my husband, remember me? Does he think of me?". Hanumaan answered every question and then he said "Mata, now I have to go. I have some work to do here". Sita held the ring close to her and sat down.

Hanumaan was very hungry and destroyed some trees in Ashok Vatika and ate many fruits. The guards rushed to Ravan. He asked, "Soldiers, go and stop that vanar". But the soldiers returned wounded, beaten by Hanumaan. Next, Ravan sent more and more soldiers as Ashok Vatika became more full by the moment covered with dead bodies killed by Hanumaan. Finally, in anger, Ravan sent his younger son, Akshay. Hanumaan killed Akshay. When the news reached Ravan, he was heartbroken. Indrajit, Ravan's elder son said "I will go, father. I will take revenge for my younger brother. I will bring that vanar captive". Indrajit went and fought with Hanumaan, for a long time. Finally, Indrajit used his Brahmastra weapon which seized Hanumaan. Indrajit took away Hanumaan. In Ravan's court, Ravan asked in the presence of all his ministers, Indrajit and Vibhisan to Hanumaan "Who are you? What is your name?". Hanumaan said, "My name is Hanumaan and I am a slave of Lord Rama". Ravan thundered "What! Ram, that hermit. Oh! The husband of Sita, right. You killed my son and many soldiers and dared to destroy my favorite garden, Ashok Vatika".

Ravan decided to kill Hanumaan but Vibhisan told Ravan that killing somebody's messenger is not the right thing to do. So, Ravan decided to burn Hanumaan's tail, the most priced possession of any other vanar, their tails. But when Hanumaan's tail caught fire, he flew all around Lanka and burned all the houses and the whole palace. Ravan watched as his golden kingdom was reduced to ashes. Then Hanumaan washed his tail in the sea and flew back to Sita. Sita gave him a hair ornament. Sita also told Hanumaan "Once, Indra in the form of a bird pecked at my feet. I was in pain. Ram aimed an arrow at him. Unable to save himself, he bowed down for forgiveness.

Ram forgave him but made a small hole in his eye. Tell this to my Lord. He will believe that you have reached here as nobody except I and he knew about this. Now you may go". Hanumaan flew back. Jambhavan, Angad, and Hanumaan along with everyone else went back to Sugreeva, Ram, and Lakshman. Hanumaan gave Sita's jewel to Ram and told the story also. Ram, Lakshman, Hanumaan, and Sugreeva along with the whole vanar army marched towards the seashore. They reached there. They had put tents on the seashore.

There in Lanka, Vibhisan would constantly convince Ravan to return Sita to Ram but he never listened to him. Finally, irritated, Ravan banished

Vibhisan from Lanka. Vibhisan went to his mother, Kaikesi, bid her farewell, and with 2-3 ministers left for Ram. Vibhisan along with his ministers flew using their demonic powers and reached the other side where Ram was camping. Ram welcomed him and asked him. Vibhisan explained everything and then he said "Lord, from today I will support you even if I have to be the friend of my brother's enemy. I will stay with you". Ram said, "My friend, after killing Ravan, I will appoint you as the king of Lanka". Sugreev asked, "But Lord, if Ravan comes falls at your feet, begs for forgiveness, and returns Mata Sita, then what will you do?". Ram said, "If that happens, I will make Vibhisan the king of Ayodhya as for me, a Suryavanshi, we always keep a promise". Ram did the crowning of Vibhisan for the future.

Vibhisan suggested Ram pray to the sea god. Ram sat in deep meditation. The sea god appeared and said, "Nal and Neel will help you". Nal and Neel were the sons of the twin Ashwini Kumars. They were also vanars. They put stones on the sea which floated on the surface. Hanumaan would write Jay Shri Ram on every stone and the vanars would carry them to Nal and Neel who would throw the stones down which would float and construct a bridge. Finally, after many days the bridge to Lanka was constructed. Ram was highly pleased. Then, Ram, Lakshman, Hanumaan, Sugreev, Vibhisan, and the whole vanar army walked crossing the bridge. After a few days, of walking, they reached the outskirts of Lanka. There, they put up tents. The place where they were camping was just a few miles away from Lanka.

Ram wanted to give Ravan a last chance. So, he sent Angad to Ravan for a peace message. Angad flew and entered Lanka. He was led to Ravan's court by his ministers. Ravan asked, "Who are you and why are you here?". Angad said "My name is Angad. I am Bali's son who has been killed by Ram. Don't you remember that you had been in my father's arms for years because of a fight? You pleaded to forgive you so he let you go. I am from Lord Ram's army and I have come here for a peace message according to my Lord. Ravan said, "You are my friend Bali's son yet you support Ram even when he killed your father. Angad, be on our side. Leave Ram and we will together kill Ram and take revenge for my friend and your father's death". Angad said, "My father had done a wrong thing with Uncle Sugreev. And I will be sorry to tell you Ravan that I will never leave my beloved Lord Ram and join a sinner like you who takes away a woman by force". Ravan refused to accept the peace message so Angad went away flying.

10. WAR BEGINS

Ram and the Vanar army were prepared for war. The next day the conch blew as both armies stood on the battlefield. The war started. Hanumaan and Sugreev killed many of Ravan's fierce warriors. Day by day passed and the fight was going in favour of Ram. Every day, a lot of Ravan's warriors were killed. Finally, Ravan tried to wake up Kumbhkarna, his younger brother who had a boon from Lord Brahma that he would sleep till 6 months then he would wake up and eat then again he would go to sleep. Kumbhkarna was very tall and big. Ravan waked up Kumbhkarna. When he came to know that Ravan had brought Sita and kept her captive and a war was going on, he immediately went to Ravan. Kumbhkarna tried to reason with Ravan and told him to return Sita but Ravan was adamant. So, Kumbhkarna went to war.

11. FALL OF INDRAJIT AND KUMBHKARNA

Kumbhkarna walked as thousands of Vanars were crushed under his feet. Finally, Ram had to fight with him. Ram first cut Kumbhkarna's arms then his head. Kumbhkarna was dead. Ravan became very sad because he had lost a companion and his younger brother. Seeing his father worried, Indrajit went to war. He disappeared using his Maya (magic and illusion) powers. Ram and Lakshman together faced Indrajit. Indrajit fired two snake arrows which got wrapped around Ram and Lakshman. They both became unconscious and fell. Hanumaan and Sugreeva picked them up and took them away. Hanumaan flew to Garuda (the bird on which Lord Vishnu travels) and asked him for help. Garuda immediately came and cut the snake ropes and Ram and Lakshman became well again.

The next day, Indrajit and Lakshman fought when Indrajit fired an arrow which made Lakshman unconscious. Ram was deeply saddened by this. Hanumaan brought a doctor from Lanka who said to bring a herb Sanjeevani from the Himalayas. Hanumaan flew at great speed but could not recognize the plant so he brought the whole mountain of herbs. The doctor gave the right medicine to Lakshman and he woke up completely well.

The next day before going to war, Indrajit also tried to convince Ravan that Ram was Lord Vishnu and that he should return Sita but Ravan was not even ready to listen. Indrajit went away to war. Lakshman again fought with him and this time Lakshman cut Indrajit's head. Indrajit was dead. Ravan was very sad this time losing his mighty son.

12. DEATH OF RAVAN

The next day was the final day of the war as Ravan and Ram were going to fight. Ravan and Ram fired arrows continuously. Vibhisan came towards Ram and said, "Lord, shoot an arrow on his stomach. All his powers lie there. He will surely die". Ravan fired an arrow towards Vibhisan angrily but Vibhisan flew down he got saved. After that, Ram fired an arrow on Ravan's stomach. Ravan fell dead. Finally, the war was over. Mandodari along with many ministers came running and cried for Ravan's death. Ram appointed Vibhisan as the new king of Lanka.

Sita was brought to the place where Ram, Lakshman, and the whole vanar army had put up tents. But Sita had to pass the Agni Pariksha (fire test). It was because much time before when Sita was not even taken away by Ravan, Ram had known what was going to happen. So, they called Agni Dev who kept the real Sita and produced a duplicate but exact copy of the real Sita. So, to gain the real Sita, this Sita had to go into fire. Lakshman produced a burning fire flame in which Sita went. Agni Dev appeared with the real Sita. Ram was very happy and he welcomed his wife after so many days of separation.

Ram, Sita, Lakshman, Hanumaan, Vibhisan, Sugreev, Angad, and Jambhavan all went back to Ayodhya in Puspak Viman. Ram was crowned as the king of Ayodhya. Ram ruled over Ayodhya for many years respecting all rules of righteousness. Everyone in his kingdom lived happily. Here ends the 7th avatar ofLord Ram.

Test Your Knowledge

Q1. How many wives did King Dasharath have?

a. 3
b. 4
c. 5
d. 1

Q2. How many sons did Dasharath have altogether?

a. 5
b. 10
c. 4
d. 3

Q3. What was the name of Ravan's sister?

a. Shoorpanakha
b. Mandodari
c. Kaikei
d. Sumitra

Q4. In which flying vehicle did Ravan take away Sita?

a. Aeroplane
b. Helicopter
c. A flying chariot
d. Puspak Viman

Q5. Which brother of Ravan became a friend of Ram?

a. Vibhisan
b. Kumbhakaran
c. Indrajit
d. Kuber

8
Krishna Avatar

1. KRISHNA IS BORN

Many years ago, there was a kingdom, Mathura which was ruled by King Ugrasena. He had a son named Kansa. But Kansa was not good-natured, helpful, loving, or caring like his father. Instead, he was cruel and killed many helpless people and animals. He was too impatient to become the king so he put Ugrasena in jail and became the King of Mathura. Kansa loved his cousin sister, Devaki, very much. He had her married to his friend Vasudeva.

Kansa was just taking Devaki and Vasudeva in a chariot after their marriage when a heavenly voice was heard. It said, "Kansa, Devaki's eighth child will kill you". An angry Kansa, immediately wanted to kill Devaki but Vasudeva pleaded with him to spare Devaki and promised him to give all the eight sons of Devaki one by one. Kansa was convinced and he put Vasudeva and Devaki in prison. Soon, Devaki's first son was born. Kansa immediately came and cut the newborn's head. Devaki watched helplessly as her 6 sons were killed.

When her seventh child was in her stomach, she really wanted that this son should be saved. She prayed to god and Goddess Yogamaya shifted the seventh child from the stomach of Devaki to Rohini, the first wife of Vasudeva. He was named Balaram. So everyone in Mathura including Kansa thought that due to some problem, the seventh child of Devaki was killed in her stomach itself. When the eighth child was expected to be born, Kansa became very alert. On the eighth day (Ashtami) of the dark fortnight, Devaki gave birth to Krishna who was the eighth avatar of Lord Vishnu. A heavenly voice said "Now, Vasudeva, in the nearest village Gokul, your friend Nanda and his wife Yashoda have given birth to a baby girl. Get out of this palace, cross the Yamuna and keep this boy there, and bring the girl here". First, Vasudeva was scared but when Yogamaya opened his chains, all the guards suddenly went into a deep sleep and the gates of the prison opened, Vasudeva carried the newborn child in a basket on his head and walked out of Mathura. He was soon standing before the Yamuna.

Vasudeva started walking across the river as clouds gathered and it began to rain tremendously. Soon the water began to rise and Vasudeva was no longer able to breathe. Yamuna again went down and spoke "Vasudeva, don't be scared. I just wanted to touch the feet of Lord Krishna". Sheshnaag, the serpent appeared and spread all his hoods over Krishna and Vasudeva to protect them from the rain. After walking for a long time, Vasudeva finally reached Gokul where Nanda lived.

Vasudeva entered Nanda's house quietly, kept Krishna near Yashoda, and brought the baby girl. He returned to Mathura, tied the chains around him and the guards soon woke up hearing the baby girl's cry. Kansa entered the prison. He said, "Hand me the child". When Devaki gave him the baby girl, Kansa laughed "What! A girl born to kill me? Ha! Ha! Ha!". He was about to smash the girl's head when the girl flew from his hands and went outside the window. The girl became Goddess Yogamaya. She appeared in her divine form and said "Kansa! Your enemy has taken birth somewhere else. Your end is near. You tried to kill me? Remember this Kansa, the more you kill people and trouble innocent people and animals the nearer your death will come to you". Kansa glared at Devaki and walked away to his room. He couldn't sleep that night. He was just worried about the words of Yogamaya.

2. CHILDHOOD ACTIVITIES

The entire Gokul was celebrating the birth of the son of their village chief, Nanda. Everyone in the village came to just have a look at the handsome, cute boy. All the villagers brought food, sweets, gifts etc for the newborn. Slowly, slowly Krishna began to grow. One day Rohini came to Nanda's house with Balram. Balram was very excited to see his younger brother. Rohini gave baby Krishna a peacock feather which Rohini placed on Krishna's hair. Since then, Balram began to live with Krishna.

Kansa was very angry. One of his ministers advised him to send Putana, a demoness, to kill Krishna. The minister said that Putana had poisoned chests and he said Putana would feed all the newborns in Mathura so that Krishna would also be killed. Putana had killed many children and was marching towards Gokul. She changed her big demoness form into a very beautiful woman. She entered Nanda's house and said that she was a goddess. She told Yashoda that she wanted to feed him. Yashoda was enchanted by her beauty and believed her. But instead of drinking milk, Krishna bit her chest very hard and Putana fell down dead in pain. Yashoda fainted seeing the big demoness. But when Krishna came unharmed, she was relieved. Soon after Kansa sent many more demons- Aghasura, Bakasura, and many other demons. But Krishna killed all of them single-handedly.

Once an old woman was selling mangoes. Krishna who now was able to crawl and stand saw that the old woman was calling out but nobody was buying from her. Exhausted the woman fell under a tree. Krishna went to her and asked for some mangoes. The woman smiled and gave him some and asked him to pay. Krishna went to Yashoda and brought some rice in his tiny palms. When he returned, most of the rice grains had fallen from his palms and only a few remained. Krishna was sad and disappointed. The old woman smiled at his innocence and took the grains and filled Krishna's palms with some more mangoes. Baby Krishna went away happily. But to the old woman's surprise, when she reached home to found that the basket in which she had stored mangoes was filled to the top with gold, diamonds, precious necklaces, bracelets made with pearls, gold bangles, etc.

The elders of Gokul experiencing all these events thought that some evil powers had come to Gokul. So, they decided to move to a better place. Balram and Krishna were a bit sad because they were about to miss Gokul. Everyone left Gokul and they made Vrindavan their new home. Balram and Krishna spent their childhood days, playing and dancing with their friends.

3. KILLING KANSA

Krishna and Balram grew up and became strong. Krishna was also an expert in playing his flute. All the villagers of Vrindavan stopped their work just to listen to the pleasant sound of the flute when Krishna played it. One day a man came and invited Krishna and Balram to Mathura. Yashoda did not want her son to go as she knew that Kansa wanted to kill his son and even if Krishna survived, he would never come back to Vrindavan again and live with Devaki and Vasudeva as they were his real parents and they would not let Krishna come back to Vrindavan.

But Krishna said "Mother, it's time for me to finish one work for which I was born. It was wonderful to have you and Dad as my beloved parents till now. But Mom I will have to depart now with brother Balram. Don't worry Mother Yashoda, I will always remember you and miss you as you will miss me. Sorry Mother, but I have to go". Saying these words, Krishna and Balram packed some food, and clothes and went away as Nanda consoled the crying Yashoda.

When Krishna reached Mathura, he and Balram decided to explore the beautiful city. Krishna saw a washerman carrying a bundle of clothes. When Krishna asked for some clothes the washerman said "Boy, go away from here. I won't give you any clothes. These new and beautiful clothes are for King Kansa and not for a poor cowherd boy like you". Krishna got hold of the washerman's head and threw him down. The attendants ran away in fear. Krishna picked up a yellow robe while Balram wore a blue one. They asked a tailor to design their robes who was happy to do so. Krishna blessed him with a long and healthy life. Then Krishna saw a beautiful woman but she was bent down on three sides of her body. She was carrying sandalwood paste. Krishna asked, "Lady, will you please put some paste on my and my brother's forehead?". The woman smiled and said, "This is for Kansa. I was carrying it for him but you both are more deserving". She put the paste on Krishna's and Balram's foreheads. Krishna said, "Thank you, beautiful woman".

Suddenly the woman looked sad. She said "Shree Krishna, I had thought that you were kind and caring to all. But now I feel that you are not. When the world makes fun of me and hates me why would you be an exception and praise me as a beautiful woman? You know that I am ugly to look at so you are making fun of me". Krishna said, "Who said that you are ugly?". Krishna put his foot on the woman's feet, pressed it gently, lifted her chin and soon her body was straight like any other woman. She thanked Krishna and apologized for her rude words.

Krishna soon entered Mathura's palace with Balram. A wrestling match was going on. Chanura and Mustika, the best wrestlers of Mathura challenged Krishna and Balram who instantly killed them. Kansa was enraged and ordered to kill Devaki but Krishna leapt on him and fought with him. In his last moments of life, Kansa saw Krishna in his divine Vishnu form. Krishna killed Kansa who went into Krishna's body. Krishna and Balram ran to the prison and freed their parents, Devaki and Vasudeva along with their grandfather King Ugrasena.

King Ugrasena became the king of Mathura and ruled wisely as Devaki and Vasudeva sent Balram and Krishna to Sage Sandipani's ashram for study. In the ashram, Krishna became very close friends with Sudama. When Sandipani's teaching came to an end Krishna said "Guru, ask for any gurudakshina (In olden times, when the teaching of a teacher to a student gets over, the teacher asks the student to give something which is called gurudakshina)". The sage did not desire anything but his wife asked to bring back their son who had disappeared mysterically. Ram and Balram went to Lord Yama, The God Of Death. But he said, "I have not taken Sage Sandipani's son. In fact the water asura has swallowed him". Krishna fought and killed the asura and brought back the child. Then Krishna and Balram came back to Mathura.

4. CONSTRUCTION OF DWARAKA

Jarasandh who was the father-in-law of Kansa was very angry as his daughters were left alone after the death of Kansa. He attacked Mathura for 17 times to take revenge. He hated Krishna very much. One day, in Mathura's royal court, Balram said "It seems as if Jarasandh is going to attack us again". Krishna said, "I have a good idea. Let's leave Mathura and shift to a new place and stay there". The ministers said proudly "Never! We have stayed here from the beginning of our life and will stay here till our death. We will fight if needed but never shift to another place". Ugrasena said, "Silence! Whatever my grandson says has a specific reason. It's my final decision that we will move. But Krishna where will we go?". Then Krishna smiled and Vishwakarma, The Architect Of Gods came. He showed the layout of a wonderful kingdom called Dwaraka which he had made and Dwaraka was surrounded by seas. In a few days, Ugrasena, Balram, Krishna, Devaki, Vasudeva, and all the people and ministers of Mathura went to Dwaraka and lived happily for some days.

In the meantime, one of Krishna's aunt had given birth to an ugly baby with a very bad-looking face and with 4 arms. His name was Shishupala. Shishupala's mom was very upset with her ugly baby boy. She called physicians, doctors, and scientists but nobody could cure him. A sage went to her and said "Very soon, a person will come and as soon as your child sits on his lap, your child's arms and ugly look will go away. But that person will also be the cause of Shishupala's death". Soon, Krishna, Devaki, and Balram went to visit. Shishupala's extra arms fell out as soon as he sat on Krishna's lap. Krishna's aunt was very sad. She called Krishna and begged him to forgive her son but Krishna said "If it is destined that he will be killed by me, I will have to kill him even if he is my brother. But still, I can give him a chance. I will give him 100 chances. The day he makes 100 mistakes, I will kill him. My counting starts now".

5. MEETING WITH THE PANDAVAS

There the five Pandavas (also the cousins of Shree Krishna), Yuddhisthira, Bheema, Arjuna, Nakul, and Sahadev had escaped the wax house fire safely with their mother Kunti and were roaming here and there in the jungle. They lived for a few days in a village but then they made a small mud hut on a vast field of land and stayed there happily for a few days. In the morning,

Yuddhisthira, Nakul, and Sahadev would beg from one house to another for alms and Bheema and Arjun would sit outside temples doing the same. In the evening the brothers would give the alms to Kunti who would cook the rice and everyone would have a small portion of it.

Just near their cottage was a kingdom Panchala, which was ruled by king Drupada. King Drupad was Drona's enemy. Drupad had made a yagna (fire ritual) to get a son who would kill Drona. Out of the burning fire emerged Dhrishtadyumna and along with him emerged Draupadi. They both, brother and sister were loved by their father Drupad, and their brother Shikandi. Now Drupad was holding a swayamvara for Draupadi.

The five Pandavas went to see what was happening as they were expecting to get some alms. In Panchala's court, Duryodhana, Dushasan, Shakuni and Karna were present. Krishna who was also there with Balram as he was a good friend of Draupadi recognized the Pandavas. Extremely beautiful Draupadi was sitting on a chair holding a garland of flowers. There was a small bowl of water in the middle of the room and a big bow on the table. There was also an artificial toy fish moving on the top of the wall. The rule was that the one who would shoot the fish's eye only by looking at the reflection of it in the water would marry Draupadi. All the kings and princes along with Duryodhan and Dushasan could not even pick the bow. Karna did but Draupadi stopped him from shooting as she did not want to marry the son of a charioteer. Finally, Arjun wanted to take part but all the kings opposed him as he was a Brahmin (in disguise). But Arjun took part with the permission of Drupad and succeeded. Draupadi married Arjun.

The five Pandavas took Draupadi to their cottage. Arjun said jokingly "Mother Kunti, we have brought some alms". Kunti said without looking back "Distribute it among your brothers". The five Pandavas were dumbfounded. In the meantime, Drupad had sent Dhrishtadyumna to find out more about his son-in-law. Kunti saw back and regretted her words. She walked over and asked sternly "Arjun, why did you joke about this beautiful girl? She looks like a princess. Who is she?". Draupadi bowed to Kunti and explained everything. Yuddhisthira said, "Mother, we are worried. You said to distribute her. But how can we do that?".

Just then Krishna reached there. He said, "Aunt Kunti, namaste (a greeting done to elders by joining palms in Indian culture). Don't worry. It is written in Draupadi's fate that she will marry the 5 Pandavas". Dhrishtadyumna ran to Drupad and reported everything. Drupad was truly happy that his daughter had married those 5 brave and powerful warriors.

He called his sons-in-law and asked how they had survived the wax house fire. The 5 Pandavas explained everything. Drupad was very happy knowing that his daughter had married the five strong, brave, and wise Pandavas as he wished.

6. THE GAME OF DICE

After some days, Dhritarashtra consulted with Vidhura and Bheeshma and decided to call back the Pandavas. The Pandavas returned to Hastinapur along with Draupadi and Kunti. They were welcomed by the people with great joy and happiness. A meeting was held where it was decided that a portion of Hastinapur should be given to the Pandavas to rule. So, Dhritarashtra gave Khandavprahasth, a large barren land. The five Pandavas went there and built a palace and named it Indraprastha. The palace was extraordinary under the guidance of Lord Krishna. They lived happily for many days. Yuddhisthira even performed the Raj-Suya yagna after Bheema killed Jarasandh. In the Raj-Suya yagna Krishna killed Shishupala using his Sudharshan Chakra because he insulted Krishna many times and crossed the limit of 100.

Duryodhana was very jealous with envy. So Shakuni invited Yuddhisthira to a game of dice. Yuddhisthira lost everything he staked-horses, jewellery, chariots, elephants, Indraprastha. Finally, he began to stake his brothers one by one. He lost them and then he staked himself and lost himself too. Shakuni convinced him to stake Draupadi. The elders watched in silence how Draupadi was staked, and then lost. Duryodhan laughed and said "Bring Draupadi here.". Dushasan went there and dragged her to the court by her hair forcefully. Draupadi was crying and pleading for help. Duryodhan said, "Take off her clothes, Dushasan". Dushasan took one hold of Draupadi's sari and began to take it off. Draupadi prayed to Lord Krishna. Lord Krishna helped her by giving more and more sari. Dushasan kept on removing her sari but it never came to an end. This was the miracle of Lord Krishna. Dhritarashtra returned everything to Yuddhisthira and the Pandavas went back to their kingdom and lived happily.

But Duryodhan was not satisfied. He again invited Yuddhisthira to a game of dice and again he accepted. But this time Duryodhan said, "Brother Yuddhisthira, if you lose you have to stay in the jungle for 12 years and one more year you have to hide. If you are found by our men, you will have to live more 12 years". Yuddhisthira accepted the rule but lost the game.

The five Pandavas along with Draupadi went to live in the jungle. Slowly, slowly the 12 years came to an end. Arjun said, "I think we can live in Matsya, King Virat's kingdom". So Yuddhisthira disguised himself as a game entertainer and advisor to King Virat with the name Kanka. Bheema became a cook, Ballav. Arjun became an eunuch, Brihanalla, and trained the princess to dance. Nakula became Granthika and grazed horses. Sahadeva became Tantipala and grazed cows and Draupadi became Sairandhri and became the maid servant of the queen. King Virat had one daughter and one son. His son was Uttara and his daughter's name was also Uttara.

One day the commander-in-chief, Keechaka tried to force Draupadi into his room. At night Draupadi wept and complained to Bheema. Bheema made a plan. The next day, Draupadi apologized to Keechaka and told him to be present in the dining hall. Bheema wore the dress of a woman and went there. Keechaka mistook him to be Draupadi and Bheema killed him. The news of Keechaka's death reached Hastinapur. Duryodhan, Dushasan, Karna, and Shakuni immediately gathered around. Shakuni said, "A mighty and powerful man like Keechaka can't be killed so easily. I think Bheema has done all this". Duryodhan and the others decided that they would seek friendship from Susharma the king of Trigarta and attack Matsya because they knew that if the Pandavas were hiding there it was sure that they would help King Virat to fight and thus they would be found out in the thirteenth year.

News reached Matsya that Susharma was ready for battle against them. Yuddhisthira and Ballav offered to help. King Virat was surprised at the exceptional strength of his advisor and cook. They defeated Susharma easily but Yuddhisthira let him go alive because he was very kind. King Virat along with Kanka, Ballav, and the entire army were resting and enjoying their victory. Back in Matsya, it was informed that Duryodhan of Hastinapur was ready for war with great warriors. Uttara, the prince, son of King Virat confessed that if he had a good charioteer, he could defeat all the great warriors. Sairandhri (Draupadi) said, "Prince, Brihanalla (Arjuna) is an excellent charioteer with great skills". Uttara said "An eunuch!". But when Brihanalla came riding the chariot Uttara could not back out. He went to the battlefield. But, at the first sight of the great warriors of Hastinapur, Uttara jumped out and tried to run away but Arjuna caught him and told him to ride the chariot. Arjun fought for him and defeated the warriors. Both of them went back in victory.

The next day the five Pandavas and Draupadi wore their original clothes and revealed who they truly were. King Virat apologized to them if he had insulted them in any way. Back in Hastinapur, Duryodhan said "More 12 years for the Pandavas! We discovered Arjuna!". But Bheeshma said, "No, Duryodhan. You are completely wrong. When we saw Arjun 13 years had passed away. Now you must return their kingdom to them". Duryodhan shouted "Never! I will never return back their kingdom. We will fight if it is needed but I will never return Indraprahastha".

7. THE MAHABHARAT WAR

Yuddhisthira did not like the idea of war so he asked Krishna to go to Hastinapur and ask for Indraprastha. Yuddhisthira said, "Lord Krishna, not Indraprahastha. Just ask for 5 villages". Krishna went there but Duryodhan said, "We won't even part an inch of our soil". Krishna came back and said, "No, Duryodhan did not listen to me. He wants war". Arjun and Bheema shouted in anger "If he wants war, he shall have war". So, it was decided that the Great War would take place. Shakuni had said to Duryodhan to seek help from Krishna. Duryodhan and Arjuna reached together but Krishna said "One can have me, the other can have my Narayani Sena (Army)". Arjun chose Krishna and Duryodhan went back happily with the Narayani Sena but to his surprise, Shakuni said "Duryodhan, Krishna cannot be compared to even millions of soldiers!".

THE FIRST DAY

On the first day of the war, the rules were decided. The battlefield was famously called Kurukshetra. The commander-in-chief of the Kauravas was Bheeshma. Lord Krishna was Arjuna's charioteer. But when Arjuna saw his near and dear ones in the opposite army, he dropped his weapons and said "Lord Krishna, Duryodhan must be evil, but he is my brother. There stands my old grandfather Bheeshma, my teachers Drona and Kripacharya, the 100 kauravas. They are all related to me even if they stand against me. How can I fight them?". Thus, there began the narration of Gita by Lord Krishna. After being convinced, Arjuna stood straight and said "Krishna, I shall fight them". That day King Virat's son Prince Uttara was killed who was from the Pandavas. On the first day, the Pandavas suffered a heavy loss.

THE SECOND DAY

The second day of the war was in favor of the two great and large armies. Bheema killed many soldiers much to the astonishment of Duryodhan and Shakuni.

THE THIRD DAY

On the third day, both the armies fought bravely and killed many of their enemies. Yuddhisthira was losing hope day by day but then Arjuna appeared and said "Brother, the victory will be ours as long as Lord Krishna is on our side".

THE FOURTH DAY

The fourth day showed a clear advantage to the Pandavas as Bheema killed many soldiers and Arjuna killed Bhagadatta.

THE FIFTH DAY

On the fifth day, Arjuna killed many soldiers of the opposite army but the opposite army also gave the Pandavas a fierce attack.

THE SIXTH DAY

Drona killed many soldiers on the sixth day and the army's formation was broken. The sons of Draupadi fighted against Aswathama, the son of Drona but Aswathama was not killed by the sons of Draupadi.

THE SEVENTH DAY

On the seventh day, Nakul and Sahadeva fought bravely against the brothers of Duryodhan but couldn't harm them because they were large in number.

THE EIGHTH DAY

Bheema kills seventeen sons of Dhritarashtra on the seventh day. Iravan, the son of Arjuna fought and killed 5 brothers of Shakuni. Duryodhan became very angry and sent a demon, Alambusha, who killed Iravan. Arjuna was indeed very sad that day.

THE NINTH DAY

On the ninth day, Bheeshma killed many soldiers of the Pandavas. Arjuna told Krishna to take him to Bheeshma but Arjun fought half-heartedly, reluctant to kill his beloved grandfather. Seeing this, Krishna became angry and jumped out carrying a wheel and advanced towards Bheeshma to kill him but Arjuna grabbed Krishna and stopped him by saying "No Lord Krishna, no. You had told us before the war that you would not fight so you became my charioteer. Don't go against your promise, Krishna. I will kill Bheeshma someday or the other. That's my promise".

THE TENTH DAY

Arjuna took help from Drupad's son Shikandi on the tenth day to kill a very powerful warrior. Bheeshma had taken an oath that he would never kill a woman and Shikandi was a half-man, half-woman. So when Shikandi came to fight with Bheeshma, the old man didn't fight. But he noticed that Shikandi was firing arrows so perfectly that each and every arrow hurt Bheeshma. But then Bheeshma said to himself "Oh! That's Arjuna. He is hiding behind and firing arrows". Arjun fired and fired arrows till now Bheeshma was on the ground with a bed of arrows all around his body. Suddenly the war stopped and all the Pandavas and Kauravas gathered there to salute the great old warrior. Bheeshma had the boon of dying when he wished so he lay there waiting for the sun to change its position.

THE ELEVENTH DAY

Now that Bheeshma was lying on the bed of arrows, Duryodhana and all the Kauravas thought it best to appoint Drona as the next commander-in-chief. For 10 days Karna had been not fighting because when Bheeshma was appointed the commander-in-chief, he had told Karna not to fight as long as he was fighting. So now Karna stepped on the battlefield and killed many soldiers that day.

THE TWELFTH DAY

On the twelfth day of the war, Bheema's giant son Ghatotkach, fought against the enemy and killed many soldiers. Thousands of soldiers would get crushed as he took his giant footsteps. Many soldiers gathered around Karna and said to use the powerful weapon that Lord Indra had given him. Karna had kept the weapon for killing Arjuna but seeing the poor condition of the soldiers, Karna fired the powerful weapon which struck Ghatotkach in his chest and he fell dead.

THE THIRTEENTH DAY

On the thirteenth day, Drona formed the Chakravuya formation to trap Yuddhisthira. Susharma who was on the side of the Kauravas drived Arjuna far away from the battlefield and fought with him bravely. There the Pandavas were beginning to worry about Yuddhisthira. Only two people among them knew how to enter the Chakravuya formation and get out and they were Krishna and Arjuna who were away, unaware of the situation. Yuddhisthira decided to send Abhimanyu, Arjuna's son but he said "But uncle, I don't know how to get out".

Yuddhisthira promised him that they would enter with him but Jayadrath's powerful army blocked them. Young Abhimanyu rode through the warriors killing many soldiers. When he reached the middle point, he saw 7 people there. Drona, Kripacharya, Kritavarma, Aswathama, Shakuni, Karna and Duryodhan. They all attacked together against Abhimanyu. Abhimanyu picked a wheel and faced the enemy carrying it but the 7 warriors stabbed him and the young boy fell dead. Later that night when Arjuna along with Krishna returned to their camp after killing Susharma, they found out that Abhimanyu had been killed cheatingly. Arjun wept for his young and brave son. 7 against 1! When Arjuna got to know that Jayadrath had stood in the pandavas way and had stopped them from entering, Arjun took an oath"Before tomorrow's sunrise, I will kill Jayadrath or I shall go into fire".

THE FOURTEENTH DAY

Drona was determined to save Jayadrath on the fourteenth day. When Arjuna could not find Jayadrath, Krishna used his divine powers and made the sky dark blue so everyone thought the sunrise had passed. The Kauravas jumped out and Jayadrath came out of his hiding place. Immediately, Krishna made the sky normal (the sky before sunrise) and Arjuna killed Jayadrath.

THE FIFTEENTH DAY

King Drupad and King Virat were killed on the fifteenth day by Drona. Dhristadyumna was very angry and he attacked Drona but couldn't kill him. Bheema killed an elephant named Aswathama and shouted "Aswathama is killed!". Hearing about his son's death, Drona dropped his weapons. He asked Yuddhisthira who never lied. Krishna said to Yuddhisthira to tell that he had died otherwise thousands of soldiers would be killed by Drona. Yuddhisthira shouted, "Yes, Aswathama has been killed!". Then he whispered "Not your son but an elephant". The old teacher didn't hear the last part so he thought that his son had been killed. He sat down on the ground in meditation in deep thought about his dear son. Dhristadyumna grabbed the opportunity and killed Drona.

THE SIXTEENTH DAY

Karna was appointed as the commander-in-chief of the Kaurava Army. Bheema killed Dushasan by ripping his chest apart and drinking the blood that came rushing out. On the sixteenth day, Karna defeated all the Pandavas single-handedly and made them retreat.

THE SEVENTEENTH DAY

On the seventeenth day, Arjuna fought against Karna. Karna fired many arrows but suddenly the wheel of his chariot got stuck in the mud. He got down and tried to take the wheel out. While he was trying, Arjuna aimed his arrow. Karna said, "Arjuna, will you kill me by cheating? This is unfair!". Arjuna replied, "Wasn't it unfair when you broke Abhimanyu's bow from the back?". Arjuna's arrow beheaded Karna.

Duryodhan was deeply sad about the death of his friend. That night, Gandhari told Duryodhan to come naked to her room as she would open her blindfold over her eyes and see Duryodhan as she had a boon that when she opened her eyes, whomever she saw first, his body would become strong like steel. Krishna knew that if this happened, Duryodhan would never die. So when Duryodhan was going to his mother, Krishna saw him and said "Duryodhan, won't you be ashamed when mother Gandhari sees you naked? You are such a grown-up- up. At least cover your private part". Duryodhan covered it with a leaf and went to Gandhari. Gandhari opened her eyes but Duryodhan's thigh part didn't become strong. Gandhari scolded Duryodhan for not being completely naked.

THE EIGHTEENTH DAY

Duryodhan had lost all hope of winning after he had lost such powerful warriors in war. He went inside a lake and sat in meditation on the eighteenth day. The Pandavas reached there and told him to come out and fight. He came out and fought with Bheema. Bheema and Duryodhan fought with maces when Krishna showed Bheema the sign to hurt Duryodhan on his thigh. Bheema hurt Duryodhan as he screamed in pain. Blood came rushing out. The Pandavas were victorious in the Mahabharat War. Krishna had told the Pandavas to stay somewhere else so the five brothers went far from their camp and stayed there for the night. At night, Aswathama took Kripacharya and killed the 5 sons of Draupadi who were sleeping in the camp. Yuddhisthira was heartbroken.

The next day, Arjuna, Bheema, and Krishna went rushing. Aswathama fired the Brahmastra and Arjuna fired too. Brahma appeared there and told them not to use these weapons and take them back but Aswathama confessed that he didn't know how to take back the arrow. So he changed the direction of the arrow and fired it at Abhimanyu's wife, Uttara's womb who was pregnant. But Krishna saved the unborn. Krishna took out the gem from Aswathama's forehead which he had from the time of his birth. Krishna gave a curse "Aswathama, I curse you that you will be immortal. This is not a boon but a curse. You will wander here and there your entire life searching for the cure to your wound".

When Duryodhan was burned after his death, Gandhari burst into tears and said "I curse you Krishna. You could stop the war. You encouraged Bheema to kill Duryodhan. You encouraged Arjuna to kill Bheeshma and Karna. I curse you that after 36 years from now, the Yadu clan of yours will come to an end and you will see your dear ones fighting among themselves and dying".

8. THE END OF THE YADU CLAN

After exactly 36 years, the Yadavas fought among themselves and killed each other. Krishna lay under a banyan tree, deeply sad about what all had happened. Jara, a hunter was hunting when he mistook the heel of Lord Krishna to be the ear of a dear. He shot an arrow which pierced Krishna's heel of his leg. He cried in pain as Jara reached there and asked to be punished. But to his surprise, Krishna put his hand on Jara's head and said "You will go to heaven, Jara. There's nothing to be punished for". Lord Krishna died after some time.

This ended the eighth avatar of Lord Vishnu, the Krishna avatar.

Test Your Knowledge

Q1. Who was Krishna's actual mother?

a. Devaki
b. Yashoda
c. Putana
d. Kunti

Q2. Who was the seventh son of Devaki?

a. Balaram
b. Arjuna
c. Krishna
d. Yuddhisthira

Q3. How many sons did Kunti have?

a. 5
b. 1
c. 3
d. 100

Q4. How many sons did Gandhari have?

a. 5
b. 1000
c. 3
d. 100

Q5. Who was the wife of Arjun but not of all the Pandavas?

a. Draupadi
b. Subhadra
c. Gandhari
d. Uttara

9
Buddha Avatar

1. INTRODUCTION

Lord Buddha was the ninth avatar of Lord Vishnu who became a great spiritual leader. Lord Buddha was born around the 5th or 6th BCE in Lumbini, now Nepal. He was named Siddhartha Gautama. His father was King Suddhodana and his mother was Queen Mayadevi. Being the son of the king of the Shakya clan, he got everything his heart could wish for. He was treated using all comforts and leisure. He never had to do any work.

His father only kept him in the palace giving him all the comforts to stop him from going out and exploring the pain, sadness, and trouble of a normal person. Siddhartha Gautama married Yasodhara, a lovely princess. Yasodhara soon gave birth to a boy who was named Rahula.

2. LEAVING HOME

Even after experiencing all the luxury in the palace, his curiosity could not stop him from going out of the palace and exploring the harsh realities of life. When he was 29 years old, he finally decided to venture out of the palace. When he roamed around the city he saw four sights which completely changed his life. He first saw an old man which explained to him the reality of aging. The second sight was that of a sick man which explained Siddhartha the suffering from any illness. He saw a corpse explaining to him the pain of death. And the last sight was that of an ascetic man who seemed to be very cheerful and happy even when facing the harsh realities of life himself. This last sight inspired Gautama to be a great spiritual leader.

He understood the harsh realities of life and that this suffering could be decreased by practicing spirituality.

3. ATTAINING ENLIGHTENMENT

After that incident, one night he left the palace, his family, his wife, and his son and went deeper into the forest. He cut all his hair, gave out his royal robes, and dressed in the normal robes of an ascetic. He walked deeper and deeper into the forests for many days. He gained knowledge from many wise sages. He was in search of enlightenment. But even after gaining so much knowledge, he could not experience the great understanding he sought.

Siddhartha realized that this knowledge would not lead him to enlightenment. So, he sat under a Bodhi tree in Bodh Gaya, India, and promised himself that he would not stand up till he attained enlightenment. He sat in deep meditation. The demon Mara even tried to distract Siddhartha Gautama by creating fear in his mind but nothing could stop Gautama. After sitting under the tree in deep meditation for a night, he attained enlightenment. He got all the answers to his questions.

He understood the four Noble Truths of human life. The four Noble Truths are:
1. the harsh truth of suffering
2. the origin of suffering
3. the end of suffering
4. the path leading to the stop of suffering.

He realized all these truths and decided to share all the knowledge he got by attaining enlightenment with everyone.

4. TEACHING PEOPLE

After attaining enlightenment, Siddhartha Gautama now came to be known as Buddha. Buddha means 'The Awakened One'. He began to teach Dharma. His first teaching was held at Deer Park in Sarnath, to his five disciples. He taught them the four Noble Truths and the path to enlightenment.

He traveled to many places around India. He taught many disciples, young and old, the path to enlightenment and the four Noble Truths. Soon, everyone came to know about the great Buddha.

5. Death

At the age of 80, Buddha became ill and he realized that the time had come for him to depart the world. When he realized this, he told his disciples and followers not to depend on his presence but to follow Dharma all the time. He guided his disciples till his last breath. Buddha died in Kushinagar, India.

He was a great inspiration to all for following Dharma. He taught the path to Dharma throughout his life. He was a great spiritual leader.

So, this was the story of Lord Buddha, the ninth avatar of Lord Vishnu.

Test Your Knowledge

Q1. What is Lumbini in present day called?

a. India
b. Nepal
c. Tibet
d. Russia

Q2. What was Buddha's name before he got enlightened?

a. Suddhodana
b. Ram
c. Krishna
d. Siddhartha Gautama

Q3. When Buddha decided to venture out of the palace, what was his age?

a. 30
b. 29
c. 20
d. 40

Q4. How many Noble Truths are there in the world?

a. 1
b. 5
c. 4
d. 10

Q5. At what age did Buddha become ill?

a. 90
b. 100
c. 70
d. 80

10
Kalki Avatar

Lord Kalki is the tenth avatar of Lord Vishnu but he has not taken birth till now. He is expected to come in this Yug, Kali Yug. People believe Lord Kalki will come riding on a white horse carrying a very long sword. The seven immortals from Indian mythology are Hanuman, Ashwatthama, Vibhisan, Ved Vyasa, Kripacharya, Mahabali, and Parashurama. Towards the end of Kali Yug, society will be filled with so many evil elements even God will have trouble during his birth. The seven immortals are believed to help Lord Kalki when he will take birth on this earth in Kali Yug. Parashurama will be the teacher of Kalki. Kalki will be very powerful and strong. He will destroy all evil and establish the Dharma again. So, follow the path to Dharma. Lord Kalki is coming soon...